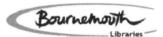

ANNE SHOOTER

# Cherish

# ANNE SHOOTER

# Cherish

### Food to make for the people you love

HEADLINE

For my family

# Contents

This book began with a request from the younger of my two daughters, Jessica, who is eleven, when she was helping me make supper one evening.

'Mummy,' she said. 'The next time you write a cookery book, rather than it being something for everyone else, please can you make it for me and Charlotte, so that when we are older we can make all the dinners for our families that you make for us.'

Yes, I know, she is super cute. And once I'd stopped congratulating myself on her loveliness (or schlepping nachas, as they say in Yiddish), I embraced the challenge.

So, in answer to my youngest's call, I've collected together all the recipes my family and friends love, and that I cook for them regularly. And it really is a collection – some have been passed down from my mum and the generations before her, others are gifts from friends, some are from my travels abroad or from meals I have eaten in restaurants and that I have been inspired to recreate at home. And, although most of the recipes have a strong link to my background – and most are connected to the fact that I am Jewish – I'm no purist and am very happy to mix in influences from all over the world to give those dishes an update for our very modern dining table. With that in mind, you'll find a happy mix of traditional recipes alongside Greek and Indian ingredients married with rich and exotic flavours from all over the Middle East and Eastern Europe.

Being Jewish basically means that food has been used to mark every significant occasion for as long as I can remember, and in plentiful quantities. ('Have some more, dolly! What, you don't like it so much?')

On a Friday night we would often go round to my grandparents' house after school before the traditional Shabbat (or Sabbath) dinner and my grandma, Freda, would be stirring the chicken soup, grating hard-boiled eggs to sprinkle on the chopped liver, and checking on the chicken roasting in the oven. Friday night always was – and still is in many Jewish families – a veritable ode to the humble chicken! An apple cake would be on a smart plate on the sideboard, next to the *Daily Express* newspaper and the whole house smelled warm and familiar. I would perch on my granddad's knee while he sat on his rocking chair watching the television, and he always let me blow out the match he used to light his pipe, relaxing after his busy week in his shop, at the time a famous kosher poultry shop on Jubilee Street in London's East End.

'Chana,' he would say to me, using my Hebrew name. 'One day, believe me, you will be a balaboosta and your own house will be like this.' A balaboosta is the Yiddish term for a wife and homemaker, a gracious hostess, a wonderful cook. And now, every Friday, like my mum, and my grandma, and her mother before her, I prepare a traditional, Jewish Friday night dinner for my family and friends – often cooking for 20 guests.

While my Friday night dinner may not be quite the same as my mother's, it is still pretty Jewish! And to explain a bit about what this means, we should understand that Jewish food basically has two sides to its family tree...

There is food from the Ashkenazi community, which is from the Jews of eastern and northern Europe. Think slow-cooked meats, salt beef on rye, smoked salmon bagels, fried fish, pies and dumplings.

Then there is the Sephardic food from Spain, Portugal, Morocco and the Middle East. This is all rather more exotic, with flavours like saffron, turmeric, cumin and citrus – dishes like tagines, stuffed vegetables, pomegranate-studded salads and pita breads filled with falafels and hummus are what this branch of the community has brought to our tables.

My own family background is mainly Ashkenazi, but much of my husband's family lives in Israel and I am hugely inspired by our regular trips there. Just recently, I explored the Yemenite Quarter near Tel Aviv's Carmel market for the first time and was introduced to some amazing new flavours in the little cafes and bakeries lining the side streets and back alleys.

Street food in Israel has always revolved around delicious things stuffed into the whitest, fluffiest pillows of warm pita – in particular, gently spiced falafel balls, accompanied by hummus, tahini, fried aubergine slices, hot sauce and endless salads, everything frantically pushed in by a server with a pair of tongs while you point at the things you want added. During my most recent visit I discovered something that looked quite ordinary but tasted out of this world – minced lamb, seasoned with salt and pepper and chopped fresh parsley, was stuffed into the bread that had been spread first with tahini, then the whole thing was fried and then toasted in the oven until it was totally crisp. Incredible! And yes, my attempt at recreating that is in these pages (try it!) along with other things I have eaten there – beautiful vegetable fritters stuffed into sweet challah rolls, breaded turkey schnitzels made into the most fantastic sandwiches with salad and pickles, chicken shawarma – made in the oven since I don't own a revolving spit! All simple, comfort foods that couldn't taste more fantastic.

As well as those two main historical Jewish influences, there are smaller pockets of communities based in countries all around the world – from India to Syria and Morocco – and luckily I have family and friends from many diverse backgrounds who often share their own traditional recipes with me. I also have a huge collection of Jewish cookery books! From the delicate Keralan fish curry to an Ethiopian chicken stew called *doro wat*, they all influence how we eat in our home and so you'll find those dishes in this book, too.

It's not exactly a bad mix of culinary inspiration to be saddled with!

So, although I will pile the table with many of the traditional Jewish recipes that my family has been making for generations, my versions just take in more of these diverse influences. I will serve chopped liver just as my grandma always did, but often with elements of a Middle Eastern mezze — a garlicky sludge of hummus; smoky aubergine babaganoush; the sultry, cooked red pepper and tomato salad called *matbucha* and a vibrant, chopped Israeli salad of cucumbers and tomatoes, perhaps pimped with pomegranate seeds, mint and parsley.

Then, there is the much revered chicken soup, the famous 'Jewish penicillin', made from simmering a chicken in water with vegetables for around three hours to produce a golden, clear broth. I always thought I made this exactly to my mother's recipe until one night at my house for dinner she commented on how delicious it was with the onions I had added that she had never used before! I love how recipes evolve like this, taking on new life with each new cook.

Perhaps one of the reasons some of those long-held traditions and preparation methods have been updated for today's table is our ever busier lives. Although I'm lucky to be able to work — at least part of the time — with food, that doesn't mean I have hours and hours to spend cooking. Like many other women, I have a family — two daughters, Charlotte and Jessica, a husband, Dan, a large labradoodle called Rufus — and a full-time job. Yet I don't buy very much pre-prepared food (unless you count fish fingers or baked beans or Ben and Jerry's ice cream or gin) and I cook pretty much every meal we eat from scratch.

I have become very good at finding meals that take little time to prepare and at creating shortcuts where necessary. I like meals I can make in advance and serve at room temperature or re-heated. I often make extra to freeze. And I am excellent at choosing dishes with a high deliciousness-to-effort ratio! With less time to spend in the kitchen, I appreciate easy meals that can be cooked in one tray — so I have included a whole chapter of those. I also like dishes that work well together and can be put in the middle of the table, or laid out on my kitchen surfaces so that everyone can help themselves when I have people over — a more relaxed way of dining that suits our family life well.

Jewish people eat a lot of chicken! And not just on Friday. So you'll find a whole chapter devoted to this glorious bird (and a few of its poultry cousins). As I said earlier, my granddad, Teddy Gold, was a poulterer and one of my favourite childhood memories is of watching my grandma cook his chickens in her kitchen, sometimes stuffed with a mixture of matza meal (dried breadcrumbs), fried onions and chicken fat. My mum always makes hers very plain, simply seasoned with salt and pepper — and sometimes (and this is delicious, however strange it might sound) stuffed with whole sausages! My own family roast chicken recipe is altogether more rich with exotic flavours — sometimes roasted with red onions and rosemary, or tarragon and oranges, or maybe with lemon and thyme.

Alongside the chicken, depending on the number of guests, there might be my acclaimed meatballs too, served in a rich tomato sauce, or perhaps brisket, cooked for hours in sweet wine with lots of onions, artichokes filled with lamb mince or a meat pie (have a look at my Middle Eastern take on the traditional version!). If you know me, you know I like to serve up an abundance for people, often way more than we need — another very Jewish tradition!

And, for me, no meal is complete without something sweet. So I'll always make dessert too – and sometimes several if I'm feeding a crowd. My sister-in-law's recipe for whiskey squares (a boozy fridge cake) is a favourite (partly because my daughters can make it for me in about 15 minutes), and I'll serve it with sliced oranges sprinkled with pomegranate seeds and mint and then perhaps a moist, crumbly walnut, orange and olive oil cake for afterwards. . .

Although Friday nights are still very much the anchor of our week and the one time we always make sure we get together with those closest to us, there are, of course, so many other opportunities to gather around the table and cherish those we care about. There are the Sunday lunches of salt beef and latkes with coleslaw and pickles, or there's my answer to pulled pork – slow-cooked lamb – created to feed a bunch of meat-loving university friends at our annual summer get-together, some of whom have children who are now going to university themselves, which is pretty scary! There are dinner parties where I might serve what I call Hampstead Garden Suburb chicken, which is a delicious take on an old-school dish called Chicken Marbella, renamed on account of it being served all the time when we visited friends when we lived in that part of north-west London.

And, of course, there are the simple everyday family suppers, like the fish stew I came up with as a way to use up the endless supply of fresh cod my parents deliver regularly from Aldeburgh, where they have a house that they go to most weekends and where I spent much of my childhood. (While researching this book I discovered that there is a Jewish version of fish stew that originates in Livorno, Italy, where the Jewish fishermen used to make it from the fish that didn't sell at the end of the week. And so, it is fish, not chicken, that is traditional for those Jewish families to eat for dinner on a Friday night.)

It's all the moments like these when food has such strong associations, marking key events and stages in our lives and those of the people I love, as well as celebrating ordinary everyday family life.

And so, in many ways, this book has been a long time in the making. Aged 40 I trained at Leiths, knowing that I wanted to turn my hobby into more than that. After writing my first cookbook, *Sesame & Spice: Baking from the East End to the Middle East*, my love for food has grown even more. I feel so lucky to be able to share that love with so many people.

This book isn't based on nonsense fads or attempts to be clever. I want this to be a book that will be widely used by everyone – whether Jewish or not – stained with ingredients, crinkled at the edges where it has been pulled down from the shelf time after time to make delicious, totally reliable, family food for every occasion.

So, here we are. The book of food that I make every day, recipes passed down, added to, made my own for my own modern family dinner table – but, although this is a book inspired by my Jewish roots, it is really simply a book of food to make for the people you love.

# Cook's Notes

- All eggs are large.

- All fruit and vegetables are medium-sized unless otherwise stated.

- All chickens are large – around 1.8kg.

- Oven temperatures are for conventional oven settings. If you use a fan oven, reduce the temperature given in the recipe by 20°C.

- When buying tahini, try to buy Middle Eastern brands, sold in plastic tubs in larger supermarkets and Middle Eastern grocery stores. Avoid jars of nasty, grey, sludgy stuff – the real thing is a paler, creamier colour. Mix in the layer of oil on top before using.

- When buying pita bread, try to find an authentic Middle Eastern brand or pita from a bakery, rather than supermarket pita breads. Supermarket pita is so difficult to stuff as it tears really easily (sprinkling it with a little water then warming it slightly, but not until it crisps, does help combat this). Pita freezes really well and defrosts quickly, particularly in the microwave, so it's worth having a stash of decent ones in the freezer!

- Matzah meal is available in many supermarkets and is made by Rakusen's. It comes in several varieties but in these recipes I use medium matzah meal. Dried, plain breadcrumbs are a decent substitute.

- Jewish dietary laws forbid mixing dairy and meat products or following meat meals with a dairy dessert. Any of the recipes in this book that contain dairy can be easily converted to non-dairy by using margarine instead of butter – I like the Pure brand. Likewise, if you would prefer to use butter where I have used olive oil, or think a dish would benefit from a spoonful of crème fraîche, do feel free to go ahead!

- On that note, please remember these are family recipes and while they have all been meticulously tested, do taste as you go and adapt to your own family's preferences or to suit what you have available to cook with in your kitchen cupboards. After all, most of these are my own adaptations of my mum's recipes!

# Soups

# Chicken soup with noodles & kneidelach

'Jewish penicillin' and, perhaps, the ultimate Jewish comfort food. I thought I made it to my mum's ancient family recipe until she came to my house for Friday night dinner just after I was married and exclaimed, 'Oh, you put onions in yours!' Sorry Mum, it's definitely better with onions. The noodles are pretty much compulsory whereas the kneidelach – or dumplings – are optional, but you really should try them. Strained chicken soup is an excellent base for other soups, from minestrone to a Thai-style soup with lemongrass and chilli. To freeze the soup, strain it first and discard the vegetables – far better to cook fresh ones in the soup, before serving.

## Serves 6–8

1 boiler chicken with giblets (if you can get one) or 1 ordinary medium chicken or 1 chicken carcass and 8 chicken wings
2 onions, quartered
4 large carrots, cut into chunks
3 celery sticks, with leaves if possible, each sliced into 5 or 6 pieces
1 leek, cut into chunky pieces (*optional*)
1 bay leaf
10 black peppercorns
3–4 flat-leaf parsley sprigs
salt
250g vermicelli noodles or dried egg tagliatelle, cooked according to the packet instructions, then rinsed and drained

FOR THE KNEIDELACH (MAKES ABOUT 15)
125g medium matzah meal
25g ground almonds (or use an extra 25g matzah meal)
150ml boiling water
2 tbsp chicken fat from the top of the soup, or use margarine or sunflower oil
2 eggs, beaten
a pinch of ground white pepper
1 tsp chicken stock powder or salt

Put the chicken, vegetables, bay leaf, peppercorns and parsley into a large pan with 3 litres of water. Bring to the boil, skim off any scum, then reduce the heat to a gentle simmer. Cook, covered, for 2½ hours. Allow the soup to cool, then carefully remove the chicken. Separate the meat from the bones and return the meat to the soup. Taste and season with salt.

Once the soup is cool reserve 2 tablespoons of the fat from the top for making the kneidelach. Then, the best thing is to refrigerate the soup overnight, so the fat solidifies in a thick layer, allowing you to remove it. Alternatively, use kitchen paper – lay a sheet on top of the soup and it will absorb the fat. Lift carefully and discard, then repeat until all the fat has been removed.

To make the kneidelach, put the matzah meal and almonds into a bowl and pour over the boiling water. Stir well, then add the remaining ingredients except the salt or chicken stock powder. Mix together thoroughly, then chill for a minimum of 30 minutes, to allow the matzah meal to absorb the liquid and firm up.

When you are ready to serve the soup, bring a large pan of water seasoned with salt or chicken stock powder to the boil. (Do not drop your kneidelach straight into the soup to cook them because, while they will taste totally delicious, you will have no soup left as they will absorb it all!) Roll the kneidelach into walnut-sized balls, drop them into the boiling water and simmer for around 30 minutes. Meanwhile, bring the soup to a gentle simmer in a separate pan.

Once the kneidelach are cooked, add them to the simmering soup. To serve, place a portion of noodles in each bowl, pour over the hot soup and add a couple of kneidelach.

# Barley soup

This is a really traditional, hearty, fill-your-boots, meal-in-a-bowl kind of soup that my daughters request the minute the weather turns really cold. It reminds me of my Lithuanian roots — it would have been a staple there, as well as in Poland and Russia. *Krupnik* is very similar but with dried mushrooms in it, so feel free to add those if you wish. I make it with beef bones or lamb neck bones — your butcher or a supermarket meat counter should be able to provide these for you.

**Serves 6–8**

75g pearl barley
50g split peas
1 large onion, finely chopped
1 celery stick, finely chopped
3 large carrots, sliced into 1cm rounds
2.5 litres beef stock (from a cube is fine)
1 large beef bone (with meat on it) or
    200g smaller bones or 200g stewing
    beef in cubes
20g dried mushrooms (ceps are particularly
    flavourful), soaked in 150ml hot water
    for 15 minutes (*optional*)
salt and ground white pepper

Put all the ingredients in a large pan, along with the mushroom-soaking water, if using.

Bring to the boil and skim off any scum that rises to the surface. Reduce the heat and then simmer for 2 hours, until the pulses are very swollen, the soup is thick and the meat is soft.

Taste and adjust the seasoning with salt and pepper. Serve warm with a little shredded meat from the bones in each bowl.

# Roasted butternut squash & chickpea soup

This recipe came about because a friend was making soup for a dinner party; she'd peeled and roasted the squash and then realised she had no red onions (which her recipe called for). Determined to continue nonetheless, she substituted the red onion with a large spoonful of caramelised red onion chutney. The result was so good that everyone in our group of friends has adopted the recipe! Here it is.

**Serves 6–8**

1 large butternut squash, peeled and cut into chunks
2 tbsp olive oil
1 onion, finely chopped
½ red chilli, finely chopped (deseed if you prefer less heat)
1 garlic clove, finely chopped
1.25 litres vegetable stock (from a cube is fine)
1 x 400g tin of chickpeas, rinsed and drained
1 tbsp caramelised red onion chutney
grated zest of 1 orange
salt and freshly ground black pepper

TO SERVE
crème fraîche
slivers of red chilli
shredded mint leaves

Preheat the oven to 200°C/Gas 6.

Toss the squash in the olive oil (reserving 1 teaspoon) and roast it in a baking tray for 30 minutes, or until soft.

Meanwhile, heat the remaining teaspoon of oil in a large pan and fry the onion over a medium heat until softened, about 10 minutes. Add the chilli and garlic and fry for a further 2 minutes.

Add the roasted squash to the pan along with the vegetable stock and chickpeas. Bring to a simmer and then cook for 20 minutes, before adding the red onion chutney and orange zest. Using a liquidiser or stick blender, whizz until smooth. Taste and season with salt and pepper.

Pour into bowls and garnish with a blob of crème fraîche, a couple of slivers of chilli and some shredded mint leaves.

# Sweet & sour cabbage soup

Whenever I hear about that awful cabbage soup diet that celebrities sometimes go on, I laugh to myself. To me, cabbage soup will always mean this amazing, delicately spiced, sweet and sour version, originating from Eastern Europe. With its sultry back notes of caraway seeds, studded with plump sultanas and enlivened with sharp lemon juice, each bountiful mouthful is more comforting and delicious than the last. Bring on that diet!

## Serves 6–8

2 tbsp vegetable oil
2 onions, finely chopped
2 garlic cloves, crushed
2 tbsp sweet paprika
1 tbsp caraway seeds
2 tbsp tomato purée
1 large white cabbage, shredded
1 x 400g tin of chopped tomatoes
75ml white wine vinegar
3 tbsp caster sugar
1.5 litres vegetable, chicken or beef stock (from a cube is fine)
3 tbsp sultanas
salt and freshly ground black pepper
toasted rye bread, to serve

Heat the vegetable oil in a large pan and add the onions. Fry gently for 10 minutes to soften, stirring occasionally, then add the garlic, paprika and caraway seeds.

When you can smell the scent of the caraway, add the tomato purée and stir to blend with everything else in the pan, then add all the remaining ingredients. Stir well and simmer for 45 minutes, or until the cabbage is really tender.

Taste and adjust the seasoning with more vinegar, sugar, salt or pepper if needed. Ladle into deep bowls, making sure everyone has plenty of cabbage as well as the broth. Serve with toasted rye bread.

# Israeli salad gazpacho with sumac croutons

This soup came about after I made a version of Israeli salad (see page 172) with watermelon in it, had some left over and decided to whizz it into a cold soup.
It was delicious – and with a few additions has become one of my favourite soups ever. If you don't have challah for the croutons, brioche or ordinary bread will do the job.

**Serves 6**

FOR THE CROUTONS
2–3 slices of challah
3 tbsp olive oil
1 tsp sumac

FOR THE GAZPACHO
8 large ripe tomatoes, roughly chopped
1 large cucumber, roughly chopped
1 red pepper, deseeded and roughly chopped
1 red onion, roughly chopped
1 celery stick, roughly chopped
400g seedless watermelon, cut into chunks
2 garlic cloves, crushed
½ red chilli, finely chopped (deseed if you prefer less heat)
100g passata
a few fresh basil leaves
a few fresh mint leaves
salt and freshly ground black pepper
olive oil, to serve

First, make the croutons. Preheat the oven to 180°C/Gas 4.

Tear the bread into small pieces. Toss in the oil and sprinkle with the sumac. Spread out on a baking sheet and cook for 10 minutes, or until golden brown. Set aside to cool.

For the gazpacho you will need a liquidiser or food processor. Whizz everything together until smooth, retaining a couple of basil and mint leaves to garnish. Season to taste with salt and pepper. Cover and chill in the fridge for at least 1 hour before serving.

Serve in bowls, scattered with the croutons. Add an extra drizzle of olive oil and a few extra basil and mint leaves.

# Minted courgette, spinach & pea soup

This is another beautifully summery soup and it is fantastic served hot or cold. The key to keeping the soup a really vibrant colour is to never let the green vegetables get too hot. If I have friends for dinner I like to serve this from a jug at the table, with the garnish already in the bowls in front of everyone. It's a really simple trick and can all be done in advance, but always gets lots of oohs and aahs. However, it's just as good poured into a mug and enjoyed in front of the telly!

## Serves 8

2 tbsp olive oil
1 onion, finely chopped
2 celery sticks, finely chopped
1 garlic clove, chopped
3 courgettes, sliced
1.5 litres vegetable stock (from a cube is fine), made up with boiling water, then cooled
200g frozen peas, plus a few extra for garnish
200g baby spinach leaves
a few fresh mint leaves
salt and freshly ground black pepper

TO SERVE
crème fraîche
lemon zest strips
cooked, cooled peas
crushed pink peppercorns
edible flowers and pea shoots (*optional*)

Heat the oil in a large pan over a very low heat and gently cook the onion, celery and garlic until softened, about 15 minutes. Add the courgettes and fry for no more than 3 minutes. Add the stock and cook gently until the courgettes are softened, then turn off the heat and add the peas, spinach and mint.

Use a stick blender or transfer the soup to a liquidiser and whizz until completely smooth; it should be a vibrant green. Season to taste. Transfer to a jug, cover and refrigerate until needed.

To serve, take individual serving bowls and in the bottom of each place a dollop of crème fraîche, a little pile of lemon zest strips, a spoonful of peas that have been plunged into boiling water and then cooled, a few crushed pink peppercorns and some edible flowers and pea shoots, if you like.

At the table, pour the soup — which can be served warm or cold — into the garnished bowl in front of each guest.

# Roasted cauliflower soup

One of the wonderful things about cauliflower and celeriac is how they both taste incredibly decadent when puréed, even with no added cream. This makes this soup perfect as an impressive light starter as well as an everyday, guilt-free supper dish. Roasting the cauliflower, along with the celeriac, gives the soup a lovely depth. Obviously, if you do want to add a swirl of cream, feel free to go ahead. It'll only make it even more delicious!

## Serves 6

2 cauliflowers, leaves removed, broken into florets
1 celeriac (about 500g), peeled and cut into chunks (if you want to do this in advance, keep it in a bowl of water to which you have added a squeeze of lemon juice to stop it turning brown)
3 tbsp olive oil
salt and freshly ground black pepper
1 tbsp vegetable oil
1 onion, finely chopped
1 leek, sliced
1 potato, peeled and diced
1 celery stick, thinly sliced
2 garlic cloves, crushed
1.5 litres vegetable stock (from a cube is fine)
freshly grated nutmeg, to taste
a splash of Tabasco (or use chilli sauce)

TO SERVE (OPTIONAL)
a handful of pine nuts
single cream
chopped flat-leaf parsley

Preheat the oven to 180°C/Gas 4.

Toss the cauliflower and celeriac in the olive oil, season with salt and pepper and tip into a baking tray. Roast for about 45 minutes, until tender.

Meanwhile, heat the vegetable oil in a large pan and sauté the onion, leek, potato, celery and garlic for about 15 minutes, or until softened.

When the cauliflower and celeriac are cooked, add them to the pan and pour over the stock. Simmer, uncovered, for about 20 minutes, then use a stick blender or liquidiser to whizz until smooth. Season to taste with nutmeg, a little Tabasco and more salt and pepper if needed.

Toast the pine nuts, if using, in a dry frying pan until they have turned golden, shaking the pan occasionally to stop them burning. Top each bowl with a few toasted pine nuts, a swirl of cream and a sprinkling of parsley, if you like.

# Fish

# Fried fish in matzah meal with tartare sauce

It was the Sephardi Jews of Spain and Portugal who brought fried fish to England, via Holland, in the seventeenth century. President Jefferson even references eating fried fish 'in the Jewish style' during a visit to London in Victorian times; fried fish also gets a mention in Charles Dickens' *Oliver Twist*.

This is one of those dishes that is made far less regularly by each generation — deep-frying at home just isn't as popular as it was — but as an occasional treat there isn't much that beats hot, crisp, freshly fried haddock, straight from the pan. It's also traditional for Jewish people to eat it cold the next day — I think it might be even better with a slice of buttered challah and a squirt of HP sauce!

## Serves 6

6 white fish fillets (cod or haddock are best because they are thick; plaice or lemon sole work as goujons)
3–4 tbsp plain flour, seasoned with salt and ground white pepper
2 eggs, beaten
about 250g medium matzah meal or other dried breadcrumbs (panko crumbs work really well)
sunflower oil (or other flavourless oil), for frying
salt

FOR THE TARTARE SAUCE
200g good-quality mayonnaise
1 tsp English mustard
½ shallot, finely chopped
3 tbsp drained and chopped cornichons
3 tbsp capers in brine (not the dry, salted kind), drained and chopped
1 tbsp juice from the cornichon jar
2 tbsp chopped flat-leaf parsley
1 tbsp chopped dill fronds
salt and freshly ground black pepper

Set up your workstation as follows: pat the fish fillets dry with kitchen paper and place on a plate or sheet of baking parchment. Put the seasoned flour on a plate next to it and next to this, a shallow bowl with the beaten eggs. Finally, put the matzah meal or breadcrumbs in another shallow bowl.

Make the tartare sauce. Mix the mayonnaise with the mustard, then add all the remaining ingredients. Mix well, season to taste and set aside until needed (it will keep in the fridge, covered, for up to a week).

Pour enough sunflower oil into a large, high-sided frying pan for it to come about 3cm up the sides. Place over a medium-high heat to heat up — you are ready to go when a little cube of bread dropped into the oil turns golden in 30 seconds. Line a baking sheet with kitchen paper.

Gently lay the fish in the flour and turn it over so both sides are floured. Do the same with the egg, then coat with matzah meal.

Using a fish slice, lower the fish into the oil and repeat until you have no more than three pieces in the pan. I wouldn't do much more than that unless your pan is huge — it will lower the temperature of the oil and stop the coating becoming crisp. When the outside is a deep golden brown — after 4–5 minutes — turn the fish and repeat on the other side. Now lift it out and place it on the kitchen paper-lined baking sheet to drain. It should be really crisp.

Once you have cooked all the fish, sprinkle with salt and serve immediately or place on a platter and keep it warm in a low oven until you are ready to eat it. Or let it cool and keep it covered in the fridge to serve cold. You can also reheat these pretty successfully by setting on a wire rack in an oven tray and warming through in an oven preheated to 180°C/Gas 4 for about 20 minutes.

Serve with tartare sauce (but tomato ketchup or HP sauce are also good).

 **Variation:** *Cut the fish into strips and make goujons in the same way, giving them a twist in the middle before dipping them in the matzah meal. (The twist helps them stay crisp by stopping them from lying flat when you take them out of the oil.) Fry them as above for about 4 minutes (there's no need to turn them).*

*You can also bake the fish in the oven. Leave out the flour and egg dipping; simply season the matzah meal or breadcrumbs with salt and white pepper, adding a pinch of sweet paprika to this mixture too, if liked, then mix with about 3 tablespoons of sunflower oil. The matzah meal should have the consistency of damp sand. Use to coat the fish fillets and then place on a baking sheet. Bake in an oven preheated to 200°C/Gas 6 for 30 minutes.*

# Keralan coconut fish curry

It was a pretty exciting moment in my life when I realised there was such a thing as Jewish curry! This recipe is adapted from one in an amazing book called *Spice & Kosher: Exotic Cuisine of the Cochin Jews* by Dr Essie Sassoon, Bala Menon and Kenny Salem, which shares the recipes of the huge Jewish community that used to live in Kerala, India. This dish, made with coconut cream and cardamom, is really fragrant, light and beautiful.

**Serves 6**

1 large onion, roughly chopped
5cm piece of fresh ginger, peeled and
    roughly chopped
1 small green chilli, deseeded and chopped
2 garlic cloves, chopped
2 tsp ground coriander
1 tsp ground turmeric
1 tsp ground cumin
350ml coconut cream
3 tbsp coconut or sunflower oil
1 tsp mustard seeds
seeds from 6 cardamom pods, crushed
4 shallots, thinly sliced
300ml fish or vegetable stock (from a cube
    is fine)
1kg skinless, firm, white fish fillets, such as
    tilapia, halibut, cod loin, haddock loin,
    cut into large chunks
a large bunch of coriander, roughly chopped
4–5 curry leaves
grated zest of 1 lime
salt and freshly ground black pepper
lime wedges, to serve

First, use a food processor to blend the onion, ginger, chilli, garlic and ground spices with half the coconut cream.

Heat the oil in a high-sided frying pan and add the mustard seeds. Cook over a medium heat until they start to pop, then add the cardamom seeds and shallots. When the shallots are golden brown, after about 5 minutes, add the spiced coconut cream to the pan. Cook for a minute or so, until the aromas start to be released, then add the stock. Cook for 10 minutes, then add the remaining coconut cream, the fish chunks and three-quarters of the coriander, along with the curry leaves and lime zest. Reduce the heat and cook gently for 10 minutes, or until the fish is cooked through.

Taste and adjust the seasoning, then garnish with the remaining coriander leaves and wedges of lime to squeeze over. Serve with steamed rice.

# Gefilte fish

When I tell people I am Jewish and love cooking, often the first question they ask me is 'do you make gefilte fish?'. The second is 'what exactly is it?'. The answers are yes, quite regularly, and gefilte fish are patties of seasoned, minced fish, either poached in stock or deep-fried in oil. They're delicious, easy to make and should always be served with chraine — a beetroot and horseradish relish you can find in most supermarkets now, or there's a recipe on page 193 — and, in my house, mayonnaise.

**Makes about 15 balls for poaching or 20 patties for frying**

1 large onion, quartered
1 large carrot, roughly diced
2 eggs
2 tsp sugar
2 tsp salt
½ tsp ground white pepper
1kg any mixed, white fish (or substitute 150g for salmon)
2 tbsp chopped flat-leaf parsley
6 tbsp medium matzah meal or dried breadcrumbs

FOR THE STOCK FOR POACHED GEFILTE FISH
a few white fish bones (*optional* — ask your fishmonger or supermarket fish counter)
1 onion, sliced
2 carrots, cut into 1cm slices
1 bay leaf
2 tsp salt
1 tsp black peppercorns

FOR FRIED GEFILTE FISH
extra matzah meal or breadcrumbs, for coating
sunflower oil (or other flavourless oil), for frying

Put the onion and carrot into a food processor and whizz until they are finely minced, then add the eggs, sugar, salt and pepper and process again until you have a smooth paste.

Now add the fish, parsley and matzah meal or breadcrumbs and pulse until you have a mixture that is finely minced but not completely puréed. Transfer to a bowl, cover and chill in the fridge for about 30 minutes so that the matzah meal absorbs the liquid and the mixture firms up.

## For poached gefilte fish

While the mixture is chilling, make the stock. Add all the ingredients to a wide, shallow pan. Half-fill the pan with cold water. Bring to the boil, then skim off any scum from the surface and simmer gently for 30 minutes.

Use damp hands to form the chilled fish mixture into about 15 balls around the size of table tennis balls. Place them in the stock and simmer gently, uncovered, for about 20 minutes. Remove the poached gefilte from the pan and place them in a serving dish, each topped with a circle of cooked carrot from the stock.

Strain the stock into a clean pan and reduce it by boiling it over a high heat for about 20 minutes. Pour a little of the reduced stock around the fish balls and, if you like, keep the rest to serve separately. Set aside to cool, then cover and chill until ready to serve. Serve cold with chraine (see page 193), mayonnaise and salads.

## For fried gefilte fish

Use damp hands to form the chilled fish mixture into
20 walnut-sized balls – slightly smaller than if you were
poaching them – and flatten them into patties. Coat them
in matzah meal or breadcrumbs.

Pour the oil into a large, high-sided frying pan to a depth of
about 3cm and heat until it is hot enough to turn a cube of
bread golden brown in 30 seconds.

Fry the gefilte fish patties in batches for around 6 minutes,
until brown and crisp – you might need to turn them to
ensure they are browned all over. Drain on kitchen paper.
Serve hot or at room temperature, either as they are or with
chraine and mayonnaise, as above.

# Sephardic fish in spicy tomato sauce with peppers

This is basically the Sephardic answer to Ashkenazi gefilte fish in that it is served on many occasions and there are endless variations. However — like most Sephardic food — it's a bit spicier and sexier and far more suited to a smarter dinner with friends than fish balls! This version is based on a recipe from a very good family friend, a wonderful cook and hostess called Marie Boorman, who has French-Moroccan roots. She adds chickpeas, which makes this a substantial main course.

## Serves 6

3 tbsp olive oil

4 garlic cloves, thinly sliced

1 tsp cumin seeds, crushed lightly in a pestle and mortar

2 red chillies, deseeded and chopped

1 tbsp hot paprika

3 red peppers, deseeded and cut into eighths

3 tbsp tomato purée

300ml water or vegetable stock (from a cube is fine)

1 tsp salt

½ tsp sugar

a squeeze of lemon juice

plenty of freshly ground black pepper

2 x 400g tins of chickpeas, rinsed and drained

a handful of coriander leaves, chopped

6 skinless white fish or salmon fillets, about 120g each

a pinch of chilli flakes (*optional*)

In a frying pan large enough to hold all the fish, heat the oil and add the garlic, cumin seeds and chillies. Fry gently until the garlic is golden. Add the paprika and peppers and continue to cook gently until the peppers start to soften. You do not want the garlic to burn.

When the peppers are just soft, stir in the tomato purée and then add the water or stock. Season with the salt, sugar, lemon juice and black pepper, then taste and adjust the seasoning. Simmer for 10 minutes, until the sauce reduces slightly, then add the chickpeas and half the coriander. Cover and simmer for a further 10 minutes.

Add the fish and continue to simmer, covered, until the fish is cooked — this should take about 15 minutes.

Taste the sauce and sprinkle over the chilli flakes if you want your sauce to have more kick. Scatter over the remaining coriander leaves and serve with challah or other bread to mop up the sauce.

# Za'atar salmon with ptitim

Ptitim is Israeli couscous — known as giant couscous in the UK, where it is now widely available from most good supermarkets. In Israel it is cooked in every family home: kids eat it with ketchup, it can be served risotto-style, it can be cooked in a tomato sauce or form the base of a salad. This recipe is so simple yet tastes really exotic — it transports me to Tel Aviv in a mouthful. It is a great, easy supper (you can leave out all the additions to the couscous and just serve it simply cooked in stock and seasoned) and it works for more special occasions, too — and the whole thing can be served hot or cold. I like it warm, served with cauliflower that has been tossed in olive oil and roasted for 20 minutes at 180°C/Gas 4.

**Serves 4**

FOR THE PTITIM
1 tbsp olive oil
400g giant couscous
600ml vegetable stock (from a cube is fine)
grated zest of 1 lemon
a small handful of chopped mixed herbs, such as mint, basil, flat-leaf parsley, coriander, dill
10 cherry tomatoes, quartered
10 pitted black olives, quartered
150g feta, drained and crumbled (*optional*)
2 tbsp pomegranate seeds
2 tbsp toasted pine nuts

FOR THE SALMON
2 tbsp za'atar
1 tsp olive oil
4 salmon fillets (skin on)
salt and freshly ground black pepper

Preheat the oven to 180°C/Gas 4 while you prepare the ptitim.

Heat the oil in a pan over a medium heat. When it is hot, add the giant couscous and stir to coat it in the oil. Cook until it starts to toast, about 2 minutes. Add the stock, bring to the boil, then reduce the heat and simmer for about 10 minutes (or according to the packet instructions). Cover with a lid, turn off the heat, and leave for a further 10 minutes, then uncover the pan and leave for 10 minutes or so to cool slightly while you start cooking the salmon.

Mix the za'atar with the olive oil and spread a thin layer on the top of each salmon fillet. Place the salmon fillets skin-side down on a lightly oiled baking sheet. Season with salt and pepper and bake in the oven for about 15 minutes, until the fish is opaque and gently flaking.

Fluff up the couscous, which should have absorbed all the liquid, and stir through the lemon zest, herbs, cherry tomatoes, black olives, feta, pomegranate seeds and pine nuts. Serve immediately, or chill and keep for up to 3 days, covered in the fridge. If you are going to so this, it is best to hold off adding the fresh herbs to the couscous until just before serving or they will discolour.

Spoon the ptitim on to each plate and top each pile with a salmon fillet.

# Salmon & cod skewers with lemon & dill

When my daughters were little they seemed more willing to eat fish if it involved pulling it off a stick! This dish is a great family staple but is also smart enough to serve when friends come for dinner. It is great with steamed couscous or buttered new potatoes and a pile of steamed green beans sprinkled with sea salt. Alternatively, serve with the ptitim on page 40.

## Serves 4

300g skinless salmon fillet, cut into around 16 bite-sized chunks

300g skinless cod loin or the thick part of the fillet, cut into around 16 bite-sized chunks

2 tbsp rapeseed or sunflower oil

a large handful of flat-leaf parsley, finely chopped

a small bunch of dill fronds, finely chopped

grated zest of 1 lemon

½ garlic clove, crushed

sea salt flakes and freshly ground black pepper

lemon wedges, to serve

You will need eight small skewers for this dish. If you are using wooden ones you can either soak them in water for 30 minutes before using to stop them burning, or cover the exposed ends with foil while they are cooking (this is what I do – I am never organised enough to remember to pre-soak my skewers!).

Preheat the oven to 180°C/Gas 4 and line a baking sheet with baking parchment.

Thread the salmon and cod cubes alternately on to the skewers. You should have two chunks of salmon and two cubes of cod on each, or thereabouts. Place on the lined baking sheet.

In a small bowl, mix the oil with the parsley, dill, lemon zest and garlic. Add a pinch of salt and a few grinds of pepper. Brush (or drizzle) the skewers with the herby oil, reserving some for brushing later.

Place in the oven for around 12 minutes. Halfway through cooking remove the skewers and brush or drizzle with the remaining oil. Remove from the oven, season with sea salt and pepper and serve with your chosen accompaniment.

# Fish fritters with sumac & tahini dipping sauce

These are fantastic to make ahead — eat them at room temperature stuffed into a pita with salad for a quick lunch or reheat and have as a starter at a dinner party. Sumac — from a Middle Eastern berry — adds a citrusy brightness and is available in the spice sections of all big supermarkets, as well as from Mediterranean or Middle Eastern grocery shops.

## Serves 4 (makes about 12 fritters)

FOR THE FRITTERS

1 red onion, chopped
1 green chilli, chopped (deseed if you prefer less heat)
1 garlic clove, crushed
1 egg
600g skinless white fish fillet (e.g. cod, haddock, hake), roughly chopped into chunks
1 tsp salt
freshly ground black pepper
1 tsp sumac, plus extra to garnish
3 tbsp medium matzah meal or dried breadcrumbs, plus extra for coating
sunflower oil (or other flavourless oil), for frying

FOR THE TAHINI DIPPING SAUCE

5 tbsp tahini
1 tbsp olive oil
½ garlic clove, crushed
juice of 1 lemon
4 tbsp cold water
a splash of hot sauce
salt and freshly ground black pepper

For the fritters, you can mix the ingredients by hand if you chop everything as finely as you can, but a food processor makes it much easier.

First, put the onion, chilli, garlic and egg in the bowl of the food processor and pulse to a coarse purée. Add the fish, salt, a few turns of black pepper, the sumac and matzah meal or breadcrumbs and pulse again four or five times until you have a textured mix — you don't want it too smooth, just make sure that everything is blended and the fish is broken down. Transfer the mixture to a bowl, cover and chill in the fridge for 20 minutes or so until it has firmed up.

Meanwhile, make the dipping sauce. Whisk all the ingredients together by hand or using a stick blender. Taste and adjust the seasoning and transfer to a small bowl.

Using damp hands, shape the chilled fish mixture into around 12 walnut-sized balls and flatten them slightly into patties. Coat each one with the extra matzah meal or breadcrumbs and set aside while you heat the oil.

Pour the oil into a frying pan so that it is about 1cm deep and place over a medium-high heat until it is shimmering but not smoking. Fry the fritters in batches for about 3 minutes on each side, or until a deep golden brown. Drain on kitchen paper and sprinkle with more sumac.

Serve the fritters with the dipping sauce on the side or drizzled over the top.

# Aldeburgh cod stew

My parents have a house on the Suffolk coast, in a beautiful town called Aldeburgh, where the fishermen bring their catch up on to the beach every morning. Dean Fryer sells his fish from a shed alongside his boat, right opposite my parents' house. My mum and dad often pop in on their way home from Suffolk on a Sunday night, with a pile of Dean's newspaper-wrapped cod fillets. This has led to Monday evening becoming fish stew night — and this is my favourite version, having evolved over the years.

**Serves 4**

2 tbsp olive oil
1 onion, finely chopped
1 carrot, finely diced
1 celery stick, finely diced
½ fennel bulb, finely chopped
    (keep any fronds to garnish)
2 tbsp sundried tomato purée
2 tbsp Pernod
1 glass of white wine
300ml fish or vegetable stock
    (from a cube is fine)
½ cinnamon stick
1 bay leaf
pared zest of ¼ orange
a good pinch of saffron strands
salt and freshly ground black pepper
about 1kg skinless cod fillet,
    cut into chunks
a handful of chopped flat-leaf parsley,
    to garnish

Heat the oil in a large, high-sided frying pan or wide, low saucepan. Add the onion, carrot, celery and fennel and cook gently over a low heat for 15–20 minutes, until all the vegetables are soft.

Stir in the sundried tomato purée, then add the Pernod and white wine, turn up the heat and bubble until the liquid has reduced by about half. Add the fish or vegetable stock and the cinnamon, bay leaf, orange zest and saffron. Turn the heat down to a gentle simmer and season with salt and pepper. Add the cod chunks, cover and simmer for about 15 minutes, or until the fish is opaque and just beginning to flake. Try to be gentle with it or the fish will fall apart.

Taste and season again if necessary, then garnish with the parsley and any reserved fennel fronds. Serve in shallow bowls, with toasted crusty bread.

# Cod with lentils

This is my regular go-to if I want fish in winter, whether as a midweek supper dish, or as a more special dinner with friends. It's the rare kind of fish dish that you can have with a glass of red wine — the Puy lentils and dried porcini nudge it towards comfort food, yet it's light enough to leave you with an appetite for cheese to follow. I sometimes serve this with dollops of Greek yoghurt to which I have added a crushed garlic clove, grated lemon zest and a pinch of sea salt flakes.

## Serves 6

3 tbsp olive oil
1 onion, finely chopped
2 carrots, finely diced
2 celery sticks, finely diced
1 small red chilli, finely chopped (*optional*)
1 bay leaf
3 thyme sprigs
75g dried porcini mushrooms, soaked in a
    little boiling water for 30 minutes
300g Puy lentils, rinsed in a sieve
700ml vegetable stock (from a cube is fine)
6 pieces of skinless cod loin fillet, about
    120g each
1 tsp smoked paprika
salt and freshly ground black pepper

TO GARNISH
100ml sunflower oil
½ onion, thinly sliced

Heat 2 tablespoons of the olive oil in a large, high-sided pan over a low heat. Add the onion, carrots, celery and chilli, if using. Cook gently for 15 minutes, or until everything is soft. Add the bay leaf, thyme and porcini mushrooms and their soaking water and stir well.

Now add the lentils and stir again. Pour over the stock and simmer gently for about 25 minutes, or until the lentils are just soft, with the slightest bite (nobody likes a crunchy lentil) and the stock has been absorbed. Keep an eye on them while they are cooking — you might need to add a little more liquid if they start to dry out. The lentils can be set aside at this point and heated up later, or you can cook the fish while the lentils are cooking.

Preheat the oven to 200°C/Gas 6.

Place the fish on a baking sheet lined with foil. Drizzle with the remaining olive oil, then season with smoked paprika and salt and pepper. Put the fish in the oven and bake for 12–15 minutes, depending on the size of the fillets.

While the fish is in the oven, heat the sunflower oil in a small frying pan until it is shimmering but not smoking. Carefully add the onion slices. They will sizzle and cook quickly — don't let them burn. Remove and drain on kitchen paper.

To serve, place a pile of lentils in the middle of each plate and top with a piece of cod, then garnish each piece of cod with a little pile of fried onions.

# Caraway-cured salmon with horseradish & beetroot

We Jews love a cured fish — be it herring, salmon or even halibut. This is one of my favourite cured fish dishes — I think of it as a Jewish riff on gravadlax. It takes the flavours of chraine (the horseradish and beetroot relish served with gefilte fish, see pages 36 and 193) and the caraway seeds of rye bread and transforms them into an elegant and dramatic dinner party starter. Your guests will be wowed — and there's definitely no need to tell them it is the easiest thing EVER to make. You just need to remember to start it two days before you want to serve it. Once made, it will last for up to a week, well covered in the fridge. If you like, you can easily make half this quantity, which I do if I am serving it on mini blinis as canapes.

### Serves 6–8

1 side of salmon (about 800g), skin on (ask your fishmonger or get it from the fish counter of your supermarket)

3 ready-cooked beetroot (packaged without vinegar), grated (use plastic gloves for this)

3 tbsp grated fresh horseradish (or use from a jar)

grated zest of 1 orange

grated zest of 1 lemon

1 tbsp vodka

a small bunch of dill, finely chopped

½–1 tsp caraway seeds

3 tbsp sea salt flakes

3 tbsp brown sugar

Find two flat (but rimmed) baking trays that fit in your fridge and are large enough to hold the salmon. Line both with cling film. (This is a precaution against leaking beetroot juice — it will stain anything it touches!)

Lay the salmon fillet on one of the trays. Check for pin bones and remove any you find.

Mix together all the remaining ingredients to create a purple sludge and spread it all over the salmon. Cover well with cling film and lay the other baking tray on top. Place in the fridge and weigh down the top tray with something heavy — tins of beans are pretty good! Leave to cure for 48–72 hours.

Remove from the fridge and carry the trays to the sink — carefully does it, as there will be a pool of red liquid around the salmon. Gently take off the cling film and remove the salmon. Scrape off the cure, rinse briefly under the cold tap and then lay on a chopping board. Using a very sharp knife, cut the salmon into the thinnest slices you can, on the bias, leaving the skin behind. The slices will have a beautiful, bright pink edge to them.

Serve with crème fraîche and slices of buttered rye, blinis or latkes (see page 174).

# One-tray Dinners

# Sea bass supper

This is a really classy dish — it is so easy you can rustle it up in no time, but so smart you could easily serve it if you had people over for dinner. The one thing to note if you are going to double up to feed a crowd, is to use two roasting trays, otherwise you will get soggy potatoes. They really are better crisp round the edges. Also, do not be scared of anchovies and capers. They are what makes this so salty, savoury and delicious.

## Serves 4

600g potatoes, quartered lengthways
   into wedges
8 garlic cloves, unpeeled
3 tbsp olive oil
sea salt flakes
3 rosemary sprigs
200g cherry tomatoes
4 x 120g sea bass fillets
1 lemon, very thinly sliced
8 anchovy fillets (in oil)
a handful of capers, rinsed
freshly ground black pepper

Preheat the oven to 200°C/Gas 6.

Toss the potato wedges and garlic cloves in the olive oil and a good pinch of sea salt. Tip into a large roasting tray, tuck the sprigs of rosemary around the potatoes and bake in the oven for 40 minutes.

Remove the tray and scatter the cherry tomatoes over the potatoes. Lay the sea bass fillets on top, skin-side down. Arrange the lemon slices over the fish, and place two anchovy fillets on each fillet, on top of the lemon slices. Scatter over the capers, season with just a little salt (anchovies and capers are quite salty already) and plenty of black pepper.

Return to the oven for 10–15 minutes, depending on the size of your fish fillets — the fish should be opaque and soft.

Serve with a green salad, if you like, and a smug smile.

# Honey & soy salmon with vegetable noodles

I have made honey salmon, as my kids call this, so many times, I am surprised they are not sick of it. But they love it now just as much as when they were toddlers. Here the veg is cooked at the same time as the fish — making it super easy. I was quite cynical about vegetable noodles when they first became fashionable, mainly because a) I actually like real pasta and b) who can really be bothered with all that spiralising? But now you can buy packs of ready spiralised courgetti and butternut squash noodles and they're really good value. So I like to use half real noodles and half vegetables when I make this dish.

**Serves 4**

4 x 120g skinless salmon fillets
4 tbsp soy sauce
2 tbsp runny honey
juice of 1 lime
1 x 300g packet of ready-cooked rice
   or egg noodles
300g courgette noodles (or 2 courgettes,
   sliced into ribbons with a potato peeler
   or spiralised)
300g butternut squash or carrot noodles
   (or 2 carrots, sliced into ribbons with
   a potato peeler or spiralised)
1 tbsp sesame oil
1 tbsp sunflower oil
sea salt flakes
1 tbsp sesame seeds

First, put the salmon fillets in a small dish. Mix together the soy sauce, honey and lime juice and pour over the salmon. Marinade for as long as you can — but don't worry if you've only got half an hour; just keep it in the marinade while you prepare the rest of the dish.

Preheat the oven to 180°C/Gas 4.

In a large roasting tray, toss together the rice or egg noodles with the vegetable noodles, sesame oil and sunflower oil. Season with sea salt and then spread them out in your roasting tray. Place the salmon fillets on top of the noodles, drizzle over any remaining marinade and sprinkle with the sesame seeds.

Place in the oven and cook for 20 minutes, or until the vegetables and noodles are hot and the salmon is opaque and flakes easily.

# Chicken with lemon, garlic & thyme with baby potatoes & carrots

This is one of those dinners that is perfect for any occasion. I often make it on a Friday night and serve it with a bowl of steamed green beans or broccoli. Every person I have shared this recipe with uses it all the time – it is so simple yet so delicious and it's easy to multiply the quantities for a crowd. It means I can whip up supper for 20 when my extended family comes round, with very little effort. The vegetables don't even need peeling!

## Serves 4

600g baby new potatoes, washed
600g Chantenay carrots, washed
2 whole bulbs of garlic, cloves separated but unpeeled
8 shallots, halved
4 tbsp olive oil
8 thyme sprigs
salt and freshly ground black pepper
1 chicken, jointed into 8 pieces, or a mixture of chicken thigh and breast pieces
2 lemons
2 tsp paprika (hot or smoked)

Preheat the oven to 200°C/Gas 6.

Put the potatoes, carrots, garlic and shallots in a bowl. Toss with half the olive oil and half the thyme. Season generously and tip into a roasting tin.

Season the chicken pieces well and put in the same bowl you have just used for the vegetables (only to save on washing up – there's no culinary reason for this!).

Grate the zest of the lemons and then juice them, keeping the squeezed halves. Mix together the remaining olive oil with the lemon zest and juice, the paprika and thyme leaves picked from the remaining sprigs. Massage this mixture into the chicken and season well. Place the chicken pieces on top or nestled among the vegetables and drizzle over any remaining marinade. Cut the squeezed lemon halves in half and add these quarters to the pan too.

Roast for 1 hour or until everything is cooked through and the chicken is browned. (You might want to move things around halfway through to make sure all the vegetables are getting nicely coloured.)

Serve the chicken and vegetables, leaving the shallots and garlic in the pan. Squeeze the lemon quarters to extract any extra juice, then discard them. Squeeze the garlic cloves with the back of a fork into the juices and discard the skins.

Pour the garlicky lemony juices and roasted shallots over the chicken and vegetables and serve.

# Chicken sofrito

Originally from Spain — sofrito comes from the Spanish *sofreir*, meaning to fry lightly — this might be the best chicken casserole EVER. The chicken is browned in a frying pan before being braised in stock, with crisp potatoes added later. In Sephardic Jewish families with roots in Spain, Portugal or the Middle East it is a popular dish for the Sabbath. My version deviates from more traditional recipes, with extra spicing and the addition of peppers, kabanos and tomatoes.

**Serves 4**

6 tbsp sunflower oil
8 skin-on, bone-in chicken thighs
150g kabanos or smoked meat sausages, thickly sliced
6 garlic cloves, bashed so they split
2 onions, sliced
200ml chicken stock (from a cube is fine)
1 tbsp lemon juice
1½ tsp ground turmeric
6 cracked cardamom pods
8 potatoes, peeled and cut into 3cm cubes
2 red peppers, deseeded and cut lengthways into eighths
4 tomatoes, quartered

Preheat the oven to 190°C/Gas 5.

Heat 2 tablespoons of the sunflower oil in a large frying pan. Add the chicken, skin-side down, and cook, in batches if necessary, until the skin is brown and crisp. Transfer to a roasting tray or casserole dish.

Add the kabanos, garlic and onions to the hot frying pan and fry gently in the leftover oil and fat from the chicken for 3–4 minutes. Add to the chicken in the roasting tray or dish. Pour the stock around the chicken and add the lemon juice, turmeric and cardamom pods. Cover the dish with foil and place in the oven.

Meanwhile, prepare the potatoes. Heat the remaining oil in the pan over a medium-high heat. Add the potato cubes and fry the potatoes until crisp on all sides; this should take about 10 minutes. Drain on kitchen paper.

When the chicken has been cooking for about 30 minutes, add the crispy potatoes, peppers and tomatoes to the dish. Cook for a further 30 minutes, uncovered, or until the chicken is very soft and cooked through.

Serve with a green salad or steamed broccoli.

# Chicken with pomegranate, walnuts & aubergine

I love serving this when I have friends over for dinner as the sweet-sour flavour is so delicious, yet it truly involves little more than putting all the ingredients in a roasting tin and popping it in the oven! It is based on the flavours of a *fesenjan* – a Persian dish flavoured with a pomegranate and walnut sauce that is often served at Jewish New Year (Rosh Hashanah) because pomegranates are said to have as many seeds as there are positive commandments in the Bible that we should resolve to accomplish – 613, in case you were wondering! I like to serve this with a simple spinach salad scattered with slivers of date and orange segments.

**Serves 4**

1 onion, finely chopped
1 aubergine, cubed
3 tbsp olive oil
salt and freshly ground black pepper
200g bulgar wheat
grated zest of 1 orange
a large bunch of flat-leaf parsley, chopped
250ml hot chicken stock (from a cube is fine)
8 skin-on, bone-in chicken thighs
150g walnuts, roughly chopped
3 tbsp pomegranate molasses
pomegranate seeds, to garnish

Preheat the oven to 200°C/Gas 6.

Put the onion and aubergine in a bowl with the olive oil and toss to coat. Season with salt and pepper. Add the bulgar wheat, orange zest and half the chopped parsley. Tip into a roasting dish, just big enough to hold the chicken pieces in a single layer.

Pour over the hot stock, then lay the chicken pieces over the top, skin-side up. Scatter the walnut pieces around and drizzle the pomegranate molasses all over the top.

Cover the dish with foil and cook for 30 minutes, then take the foil off and cook for a further 30 minutes. By this time the chicken should be cooked through and browned, and the bulgar tender. Serve garnished with the remaining parsley and the pomegranate seeds.

# Za'atar lamb chops with quinoa

This is a great one for when you've got friends coming for supper and no time to prepare! Just serve with the Tomato, Orange and Mint Salad on page 160 and some simply dressed salad leaves.

**Serves 4**

2 garlic cloves, crushed
2 tsp dried oregano
1 tsp ground turmeric
1 tsp ground cumin
1 tbsp olive oil
1 tbsp za'atar
8 lamb chops
250g quinoa, rinsed
100g dried apricots, chopped into slivers
100g roasted red peppers (from a jar),
    sliced into strips
100g pitted black olives
1 red onion, thinly sliced
grated zest of 1 lemon
a small bunch of flat-leaf parsley, chopped
750ml boiling hot chicken stock (from a
    cube is fine)
salt and freshly ground black pepper
a small handful of chopped mint leaves

Preheat the oven to 220°C/Gas 7.

In a small bowl mix together the garlic, oregano, turmeric, cumin, olive oil and za'atar to make a paste. Spread this over the lamb chops and set aside.

Mix together the quinoa, apricots, red peppers, olives, onion, lemon zest and half of the parsley and place in a baking tray. Pour the boiling hot stock over the quinoa, place the chops on top and season well with salt and pepper. Bake in the oven for 30 minutes.

Bring to the table in the oven dish and serve the lamb chops on top of the quinoa, sprinkled with the mint and the rest of the parsley.

# Frisinsal

For the Jewish community of northern Italy, there is perhaps no dish more significant than *frisinsal* — or Pharaoh's wheel. It is tagliatelle served with sausage, pine nuts and raisins — and my version uses leftover roast chicken, too — served in a round dish to symbolise the wheels of Pharaoh's chariots. In the biblical story of the Jews' exodus from Egypt, the Israelites safely crossed the Red Sea with Moses, only for the waves to close again on Pharaoh's army. The dish is barely known outside of Venice but it absolutely should be — it is stunning and tastes wonderful!

**Serves 4**

1–4 tbsp olive oil, plus extra for greasing
450g sausage meat or 8 beef or chicken sausages
100g pine nuts
100g flaked almonds
3 rosemary sprigs, leaves picked and chopped
350g (or thereabouts) shredded leftover roast chicken, with the pan juices if you have them (or use salami, cut into pieces)
500g fresh tagliatelle
salt and freshly ground black pepper
100g sultanas (golden are best, if you can get them), plumped in hot water for 20 minutes and drained

Preheat the oven to 170°C/Gas 3 and grease a round shallow casserole dish, about 28cm in diameter. A lasagne-style, rectangular oven dish, about 35 x 25cm would also be perfect, despite it being less wheel-like!

Roll the sausage meat into 16 small balls; if using sausages you'll need to squeeze them out of their casings first.

Add 1 tablespoon of oil to a frying pan and fry the meatballs over a medium heat for a few minutes to brown them. Add the pine nuts, flaked almonds, rosemary and shredded chicken.

Meanwhile, bring a large pan of salted water to the boil and cook the fresh tagliatelle for just a couple of minutes, keeping it al dente. Drain the pasta and toss it in any pan juices you have left over from when you roasted the chicken, or 4 tablespoons of olive oil. Season with salt and pepper.

Place half the pasta in the greased oven dish. Place the sausage meatballs on top, along with the pine nuts, almonds, rosemary, shredded chicken and the plumped sultanas. Cover with the remaining tagliatelle.

Place in the oven and bake for 30 minutes, or until everything is hot and the pasta has started to go a little crispy on top. Serve immediately.

# Roasted peppers with chickpeas, quinoa & feta

A roasted pepper is one of those things that can be utterly delicious or a little bit rubbish. These are so good they definitely count as dinner on their own, or can be part of a larger spread, served at room temperature. They look super pretty, too. The yellow peppers are just there to add to the colour so feel free to use only red peppers, if that's all you have. Don't go for green though — they're on the bitter side and not suited to this dish. If you want to make these but haven't remembered to soak the quinoa overnight, you can simply add 2 tablespoons of hot vegetable stock to each filled pepper half before adding the olive oil.

**Serves 4**

4 tbsp olive oil, plus extra for greasing
2 large red peppers, halved and deseeded
2 large yellow peppers, halved and deseeded
150g quinoa, rinsed, drained and soaked in cold water overnight
1 red chilli, finely chopped (deseed if you prefer less heat)
2 garlic cloves, crushed
grated zest of 1 lemon
1 x 400g tin of chickpeas, rinsed and drained
salt and freshly ground black pepper
8 cherry tomatoes, quartered
8 pitted black olives, quartered
a small handful of capers, rinsed and drained
200g feta, drained and crumbled
a small handful of mint leaves, finely chopped

Preheat the oven to 180°C/Gas 4. Grease a large baking dish.

Place the pepper halves in the dish cut-side up and place in the oven for 10 minutes.

Meanwhile, drain the quinoa well and mix together with the chilli, garlic, lemon zest and chickpeas. Season to taste with salt and pepper.

Distribute the mixture evenly between the pepper halves. Scatter each half with 4 cherry tomato quarters, 4 black olive quarters and a few capers. Drizzle with the olive oil and then return to the oven to roast for a further 30 minutes.

Remove from the oven. Either scatter with feta and mint leaves and serve immediately, or cool (you can cover them and keep them in the fridge for two or three days if you wish at this point) and then scatter with feta and mint before serving at room temperature.

Serve two halves per person for a main course or one as a starter or part of a buffet.

# Stuffed courgettes in tomato sauce

So many dishes from the Middle East and the surrounding countries are based on stuffed vegetables and there are many variants, often including meat, some kind of grain and plenty of herbs. This version is vegetarian and full of fragrant spices.

**Serves 4**

8 large courgettes

FOR THE STUFFING
85g basmati or long-grain white rice, simmered in water for 10 minutes then drained
200g tinned chickpeas, rinsed and drained
1 onion, finely chopped
1 garlic clove, crushed
½ tsp each of ground cinnamon, ginger and sweet paprika
1 tbsp pine nuts
1 tbsp currants
grated zest of ½ orange
1 tbsp olive oil
salt and freshly ground black pepper

FOR THE SAUCE
1 x 680g jar of passata
200ml water
1 tsp sugar
1 tsp salt
1 tsp sweet paprika
2 tbsp red wine vinegar
freshly ground black pepper

Preheat the oven to 180°C/Gas 4.

Mix all the stuffing ingredients together in a bowl and set aside.

Cut the stem end from the courgettes and carefully use a knife or a corer to remove the middle from them, creating a cavity for the stuffing but ensuring the skins do not tear.

Stuff each courgette three-quarters full with the stuffing mixture and then arrange the courgettes side by side in a baking dish. Sprinkle any remaining stuffing around them.

Mix the sauce ingredients together and then pour over the courgettes. Cover the dish with foil or a lid and bake for 40 minutes, then uncover and cook for a further 20 minutes.

Serve carefully – the courgettes will be ever so fragile!

# Adafina

This is a Spanish stew from medieval times, cooked overnight on a Friday and served on Saturday for lunch, to get around the Jewish laws about not cooking on the Sabbath. It is the Sephardic version of the Eastern European *cholent*, which tends to be a far less appetising sludge of beef, potatoes and butter beans. The name comes from the Arabic *dafina*, meaning hidden or buried. There are all sorts of delights in this — chicken, beef, meatballs and eggs along with chickpeas and vegetables! You don't have to include everything — but if you do, it's a real showstopper.

**Serves 8**

4 tbsp olive oil
2 onions, sliced
6 carrots, cut into large chunks
4 celery sticks, cut into chunks
6 garlic cloves, crushed
2 x 400g tins of chickpeas, rinsed and drained
4 chicken quarters (leg joints are best)
600g piece of beef brisket or chuck steak
4 beef marrowbones
8 eggs, in their shells, washed and dried
a small bunch of flat-leaf parsley
2 bay leaves
1 tbsp each of ground cumin, ground coriander, ground cinnamon, ground turmeric, ground allspice and hot paprika
5 tbsp runny honey
200g spinach leaves, washed and trimmed of any tough stalks
salt and freshly ground black pepper

FOR THE MEATBALLS
500g lamb, beef or chicken mince (or use a combination of any of them)
1 garlic clove, crushed
½ tsp ground cinnamon
½ tsp ground ginger
1 egg, beaten
a handful of breadcrumbs or matzah meal
6 flat-leaf parsley sprigs, finely chopped
salt and freshly ground black pepper
2 tbsp plain flour

Preheat the oven to 120°C/Gas ½.

First, heat the oil in a large, ovenproof 6-litre casserole dish and add the onions, carrots and celery. Fry gently over a low-medium heat for 5 minutes until the onions have softened.

While the vegetables are softening, make the meatballs. Combine the minced meat, garlic, cinnamon, ginger, egg, breadcrumbs and chopped parsley in a large bowl and season with salt and pepper. Form into 10–12 balls and roll in the flour.

Add the meatballs to the vegetables in the pan to brown them all over. Add the garlic and cook for 30 seconds or so, being careful not to burn it.

Now add the chickpeas, chicken pieces, beef, marrowbones, eggs, parsley and bay leaves. Sprinkle over the spices and drizzle with the honey. Add just enough water to cover and bring to the boil, skimming off any scum as it comes to the surface.

Stir in the spinach, really gently so as not to crack the eggs, then put the lid on the casserole dish and place it in the oven for at least 6 hours (ideally 10).

Before serving, taste and adjust the seasoning. You can give each person a bowl with some of each ingredient and some of the broth that will have formed, along with their own egg to peel. Or transfer to a large platter, peel the eggs and serve them halved, so that everyone can help themselves.

# Stuffed aubergine bake

This recipe is based on one in a truly astonishing cookery book: *A Drizzle of Honey: The Lives and Recipes of Spain's Secret Jews* by David M Gitlitz and Linda Kay Davidson. The book consists of Jewish recipes described during testimony given by household servants in the Spanish Inquisition. The recipes were known for being eaten by Jews, during festivals and on the Sabbath. The Jews who were found guilty on this evidence were convicted of being 'unrepentant heretics' and were put to death. This recipe, along with the many others in that book, attempts to honour their memory. It is truly delicious. Until I tried it, I had no idea that aubergines, apples and pears would be such great bedfellows!

**Serves 4**

2 aubergines
4 tbsp olive oil
2 garlic cloves, crushed
1 celery stick, finely chopped
1 onion, finely chopped
8 mushrooms, sliced
1 tsp chopped fresh rosemary
3 fresh sage leaves, chopped
1 tsp sweet paprika
a pinch of chilli flakes
75g ground almonds
1 apple, cored and diced
1 pear, cored and diced
2 tbsp pine nuts
juice of ½ lemon
200ml vegetable stock (from a cube is fine)
2 tsp red wine vinegar
4 tbsp breadcrumbs
salt and freshly ground black pepper

Preheat the oven to 180°C/Gas 4.

Bring a large pan of water to the boil. Drop the aubergines in, reduce the heat and simmer for 10 minutes. Remove from the pan, split in half, and carefully scoop out the middle of the aubergines, leaving the skins intact. Chop the pulp finely.

Heat the olive oil in a large frying pan. Add the aubergine pulp with the garlic, celery, onion and mushrooms. Cook gently for about 5 minutes. Add the rosemary, sage, paprika and chilli flakes and cook for another minute or two.

Add the almonds, apple, pear, pine nuts, lemon juice, 50ml of the stock, red wine vinegar and half the breadcrumbs. Cook for a further 5 minutes until the mixture starts to come together. Taste and season with salt and pepper.

Place the aubergine shells in a baking dish side by side and fill with the stuffing mixture. Add the remaining vegetable stock to the bottom of the dish.

Cover with foil and bake in the oven for 20 minutes. Uncover, sprinkle with the remaining breadcrumbs and bake for a further 10 minutes until the breadcrumbs are browned and the stuffing mixture is firm.

# Chicken, Turkey & Duck

# The best roast chicken

## (with smoked paprika, rosemary & shallots)

I make roast chicken for dinner almost every Friday night, in some form or another. The key to it is to roast it upside down for the first hour, then turn it the right way up for the last half hour. I also cook it for longer than many recipe books advise because I like it to be falling off the bone – and the breast doesn't dry out with this method.

**Serves 4–6**

1 large chicken, weighing around 2kg
2 tbsp smoked paprika
4 tbsp olive oil
1 whole bulb of garlic, cloves separated but unpeeled
1 lemon, halved
400g echalion (banana) shallots, halved lengthways
6 rosemary sprigs
sea salt flakes and freshly ground black pepper

## Variation:

*This is also fantastic with red onions instead of shallots; sage, thyme or tarragon instead of rosemary; with orange instead of lemon. The variations are endless! You can also roast whole carrots and peeled, halved potatoes around the chicken with the shallots and garlic for the same amount of time.*

Preheat the oven to 200°C/Gas 6.

Rub the chicken all over with the paprika and 2 tablespoons of the olive oil – really massage it into the joints and lift the skin away from the breast meat and rub it in well underneath. Place 3 garlic cloves inside the chicken with 1 lemon half, 4 shallot halves and 3 of the rosemary sprigs.

Place the chicken, breast-side down, in a roasting tin. Around it scatter the remaining shallot halves, the remaining garlic cloves and the rosemary. Squeeze the other lemon half over the chicken and drop it into the tin too. Season everything with plenty of salt and pepper and drizzle the shallots and garlic with the remaining olive oil. Pour a mug of water into the pan and place the chicken in the oven.

Roast for 1 hour, then remove, turn the chicken breast-side up and roast for a further 30 minutes. Lift up the chicken and pour any juices in the cavity into the roasting tin, before setting it on a board ready for carving.

Spoon off any excess oil from the pan, then squish the roasted garlic out of its skins and stir into the juices in the pan. Break up the shallots and stir them in too. Discard the lemon and rosemary sprigs. Taste the gravy and season.

Serve the chicken with roast potatoes and vegetables, with the onion and garlic gravy spooned on top.

# Hampstead Garden Suburb chicken

This is a variant on a dish that is actually called Chicken Marbella, made famous by a 1970s New York food shop called The Silver Spoon. I renamed it because there was a time, when I lived in an area of London called Hampstead Garden Suburb, that you could not go to a dinner party without it being served. It's one of those recipes that is absolutely foolproof yet looks – and tastes – extremely impressive, so it was passed from friend to friend. Now half my colleagues serve it too, I've passed it on to so many of them! I still make it regularly, with a couple of my own twists. You need to marinate this the day before you want to serve it, so it does need a little bit of advance planning. (Or you could marinate it in the morning and cook it that evening.)

**Serves 4 (can easily be multiplied to feed a crowd)**

1 chicken, jointed into 8 pieces, or
  8 skin-on, bone-in chicken thighs
2 red onions, sliced into rings
1 lemon, sliced into thin rings
100g capers (the kind that come in brine),
  drained
20 pitted prunes
150g pitted green olives, with 2 tbsp
  their brine
30ml red wine vinegar
30ml olive oil
60ml white wine
1 tbsp coriander seeds, crushed in
  a pestle and mortar
6 garlic cloves, crushed
2 bay leaves
1 tbsp dried oregano
1 cinnamon stick, broken into 3 pieces
60g soft light brown sugar
a small handful each of chopped flat-leaf
  parsley and coriander

Place the chicken, onions and lemon slices into a large bowl. Scatter over the capers, prunes and olives.

Mix together the olive brine, vinegar, olive oil, white wine, coriander seeds and crushed garlic. Pour the mixture over the chicken and mix everything around well. Add the bay leaves, scatter with oregano and place the cinnamon stick pieces among the chicken. Cover with cling film and place in the fridge overnight (or for at least 4 hours if preparing the same day).

When you are ready to cook, preheat the oven to 190°C/Gas 5.

Tip the chicken, juices and marinade ingredients into a roasting tray and arrange in a single layer with all the marinade ingredients evenly scattered around the chicken pieces. Sprinkle over the brown sugar. Roast for 1 hour, basting the chicken with the pan juices halfway through cooking.

Scatter with chopped parsley and coriander before serving with couscous or rice.

# Yemenite chicken with potatoes

When I was in Tel Aviv recently I trawled the Yemenite Quarter, near the Carmel market, and was introduced to a multitude of incredible dishes in little cafés and bakeries. This classic chicken with potato dish was one of them. It uses a Yemenite spice mix called *hawaij*, which is a heady mix of black pepper, turmeric, cumin, coriander and sweet elements like allspice and cinnamon. *Hawaij* is tricky to get hold of here so this recipe breaks it down. The list of ingredients might seem long but the spices are probably things you already have in your cupboard and it's actually a super-simple – and very tasty – dish.

## Serves 4

1 tbsp sunflower oil, plus extra if needed
1 chicken, jointed into 8 pieces, or
  8 skin-on, bone-in chicken thighs
1 onion, chopped
2 garlic cloves, crushed
seeds from 2 cardamom pods
1 tsp ground turmeric
1 tsp hot paprika
¼ tsp ground cinnamon
¼ tsp ground allspice
½ tsp ground cumin
½ tsp ground coriander
½ tsp freshly ground black pepper
5 potatoes, peeled and thickly sliced
200ml chicken stock (from a cube is fine)
salt and freshly ground black pepper
freshly chopped parsley and coriander,
  to garnish

Preheat the oven to 200°C/Gas 6.

Heat the oil in a large frying pan. Add the chicken portions and brown in batches over a medium-high heat. Set the chicken aside.

Add the onion to the frying pan – adding a little more oil if needed – and fry gently for 5 minutes. Add the garlic and all the spices and cook, stirring, for a further 3 minutes. Add the potato slices and stir around so they are coated with the spices.

Tip the potato and onion mixture into a casserole dish and pour the stock over it. Arrange the chicken pieces on top, cover the dish with a lid (or foil) and cook for 30 minutes, then reduce the heat to 180°C/Gas 4 and cook for a further 40 minutes.

Remove from the oven and taste and adjust the seasoning. Serve two pieces of chicken per person, garnished with parsley and coriander, with the potatoes and onions on the side.

 ## Variation:
*Try adding sliced red pepper, sliced tomatoes and green olives to the potatoes, if you like.*

# Chicken with saffron & figs

This elegant and exotic dish is perfect for Jewish New Year as it is sweet and fragrant, but would be delicious for any celebratory supper. Serve it with couscous and steamed green beans tossed with toasted almonds.

**Serves 4**

2 tbsp olive oil
1 tsp saffron strands
½ tsp ground coriander
½ tsp salt
8 generously sized skin-on, bone-in
  chicken thighs
1 lemon, thinly sliced
2 tbsp runny honey
8 fresh figs, quartered

Preheat the oven to 180°C/Gas 4.

Mix the olive oil with the saffron, coriander and salt in a bowl and then rub this mixture all over the chicken thighs.

Arrange the thighs in a roasting tray, with the lemon slices tucked in among them. Roast for 25 minutes, then remove the tray from the oven, drizzle over the honey and scatter over the fig quarters.

Cook for a further 20 minutes, or until the juices of the thighs run clear and the figs are softened and their juices are running.

# Oven-roasted chicken shawarma

In Tel Aviv you can barely move for shawarma — rotating spits of strips of various sliced meats, ready to be carved into a pita and topped with hummus, tahini, fried aubergine slices, chopped tomatoes, hot sauce, fried onion. . . the list is endless! This recipe brings it home, using a really easy marinade you simply slather onto boneless chicken thighs before you roast them. It's actually great just with salad or on top of a pile of rice, but for me the pita option wins every time!

## Serves 4

700g skinless and boneless chicken
    thighs
juice of 1 lemon
4 tbsp olive oil
3 garlic cloves, crushed
2 tsp ground turmeric
2 tsp ground cumin
2 tsp hot paprika
1 tsp ground coriander
½ tsp ground cinnamon
½ tsp ground cloves
salt and freshly ground black pepper
1 large onion, sliced

TO SERVE
pita
hummus (see page 184)
chopped tomatoes
chopped cucumber
pickles
olives
tahini
hot sauce

Cut the thighs into slices about 5mm thick — don't worry about getting them too thin, you can slice them thinner after they are cooked.

Put the lemon juice, olive oil, garlic and all the spices in a large bowl and whisk well to combine. Season with salt and pepper. Add the chicken slices and mix until coated, then cover with cling film and leave to marinate for at least 30 minutes but preferably overnight. (Alternatively, you can put the marinade and chicken in a large, sealable plastic bag.)

When you are ready to cook the chicken, preheat the oven to 220°C/Gas 7 and lightly grease a baking sheet.

Add the sliced onion to the chicken and stir it around. Tip the chicken and any marinade on to the baking tray in a single layer and put it in the oven for 30 minutes, or until the chicken is starting to crisp up at the edges.

Wait until it is just cool enough to handle, then cut the chicken into the thinnest slices possible. At this stage you can put it in a frying pan with an extra tablespoon of oil or remaining marinade and crisp it up further, if you like.

Serve the chicken stuffed in a pita with hummus, tomatoes, cucumber, pickles and olives, as you like, and drizzle with tahini and hot sauce.

# Turkey schnitzel sandwich

If you are a child growing up in Israel – or in my house – you will eat a lot of turkey or chicken schnitzel! You can buy it frozen, of course, but nothing beats the homemade version – particularly when slapped between two slices of challah with salad and mayo – and even more so when you know how to make it with the most perfect, moreish, seasoned, crunchy crumb. It's also delicious with mashed potato and coleslaw.

## Serves 4

4 turkey escalopes or 2 chicken breasts
   (about 700g in total)
70g plain flour
1 tsp dried mustard powder
1 tsp sweet paprika
2 eggs
120g panko breadcrumbs (or use ordinary
   breadcrumbs)
salt and freshly ground black pepper
sunflower oil (or other flavourless oil),
   for frying
8 slices of challah or other decent bread
   (ciabatta or baguette works well cut into
   4 and sliced open too, or you could use
   4 pita breads)
2 tbsp mayonnaise
2 tbsp tomato ketchup
2 tomatoes, sliced
2 baby gem lettuce, leaves separated
4 gherkins, sliced

First, prepare your turkey or chicken. If you are using chicken breasts, slice them lengthways through the breast to make two thin pieces. Take your chicken or turkey and put it between two pieces of cling film or baking parchment and use a rolling pin to gently pound and roll it until it is about 1cm thick.

Prepare the coating by getting 3 shallow bowls ready. In one, put the flour, mixed with the mustard powder and paprika. In the next, crack the 2 eggs and beat them well. In the third put the panko breadcrumbs, seasoned well with salt and pepper.

Pour oil to a depth of about 4cm into a large, high-sided frying pan. Heat until a cube of bread dropped into the oil sizzles and turns golden in 30 seconds. Dredge your escalopes first in flour, shaking off the excess, then in the egg, then the breadcrumbs, which you can press on to make sure they really stick. As you finish each one, place it carefully into the hot oil. Fry for about 4 minutes on each side, or until really golden brown and crispy.

Transfer to a rack or plate lined with kitchen paper, sprinkle with salt and set aside until all of the pieces are fried.

Now, take your bread and spread half lightly with mayonnaise and half with ketchup. Make up the sandwiches with a few tomato slices, a couple of lettuce leaves, sliced gherkins and the schnitzel.

You might want to serve with a few crisps, a cold beer and a favourite episode of *Seinfeld*.

# Chicken meatballs in barbecue sauce

I don't know when I started making these but I do know they are now such a favourite in my house that I make them pretty much every week. They freeze brilliantly – a godsend when you have spontaneously asked an extra family for dinner and your one roast chicken doesn't seem enough to feed eight. (This kind of thing happens to me A LOT.)

## Serves 4

FOR THE MEATBALLS
500g chicken mince
100g medium matzah meal
   or breadcrumbs
1 tsp English mustard
1 tbsp tomato ketchup
1 tsp hot paprika
1 egg, beaten
1 tbsp olive oil

FOR THE SAUCE
500g passata
3 tbsp soft dark brown sugar
2 tbsp Worcestershire sauce
2 tbsp soy sauce
1 tbsp white wine vinegar
a pinch of chilli flakes
2 garlic cloves, crushed
salt and freshly ground black pepper

For the meatballs, mix all the ingredients except the oil together in a bowl, making sure they are really well combined. Clean hands are best for this job.

Form the mixture into 12–16 meatballs, each one about the size of a ping-pong ball. (This is much easier if your hands are damp.)

Heat the oil in a large, lidded frying pan over a medium heat. Place the meatballs into the pan and fry for a few minutes, moving them around so they brown slightly on all sides.

Meanwhile, mix together all the sauce ingredients in a bowl or jug. Taste and adjust the seasoning, then pour the sauce over the meatballs. Bring to a simmer then put the lid on, reduce the heat to low and allow to cook for 1 hour.

Serve with rice, pasta or couscous and green vegetables.

# Chicken paprikash

When I was growing up, my mum used to make a fantastic chicken casserole, full of peppers, tomatoes and paprika. It was only more recently that I realised this was actually based on the Hungarian dish, chicken paprikash. Jewish people do not mix dairy and meat products so her version was slightly different from the original Hungarian dish, where sour cream would have been added to the sauce. Feel free to add a dollop at the end of the cooking time, if that's your thing!

**Serves 4**

1 chicken, jointed into 8 pieces, or 8 skin-on, bone-in chicken portions
1 tbsp sweet paprika
1 tsp hot paprika or cayenne pepper
2 tbsp olive oil
1 large onion, chopped
2 garlic cloves, thinly sliced
1 red pepper, deseeded and sliced
1 green pepper, deseeded and sliced
1 x 400g tin of tomatoes
1 tbsp tomato purée
1 tsp sugar
1 tsp salt
300g white mushrooms, sliced

Rub the chicken all over with the sweet and hot paprika or cayenne. Heat the oil in a large pan over a medium heat. Brown the chicken in batches, then set aside.

In the same pan and using the same oil, gently fry the onion for 5 minutes, then add the garlic and pepper slices and cook for a further few minutes.

Add the tinned tomatoes and the tomato purée to the pan, season with sugar and salt, reduce the heat and simmer for around 10 minutes, or until the sauce has thickened slightly.

Return the chicken pieces to the pan and simmer for around 30 minutes before adding the mushrooms and cooking for a further 15 minutes.

Serve with noodles or mashed potato.

# Turkey 'duck' pancakes

The UK's *Jewish Chronicle* newspaper regularly runs my recipes but I was particularly thrilled when their food editor, the wonderful Victoria Prever, called me to say she was writing an article about popular Friday night dinners and that this recipe was regularly appearing on Facebook as an alternative to the usual chopped liver and roast chicken repertoire. The truth is, I shouldn't really claim credit for it – it was passed to me verbally by my darling sister-in-law Karen, who was given it by a friend. All I did was try it out and was so wowed I wrote it down and passed it on. It's super clever. You take turkey legs (which are really cheap, particularly compared with duck), boil them and then roast them in hoisin sauce; they taste just like Chinese crispy duck!

**Serves 4–6**

2 turkey drumsticks
1 x 270g jar of hoisin sauce (I like Wing Yip, available from good supermarkets)
16 Chinese pancakes – available at many supermarkets as well as specialist stores
1 cucumber, peeled with a potato peeler and cut into thin 6cm batons
10 spring onions, cut into thin 6cm strips

Put the drumsticks into a large pan and cover with water. Bring to the boil, then reduce the heat, put a lid on the pan and simmer for 2 hours, until the meat is falling off the bone.

Preheat the oven to 200°C/Gas 6.

Remove the turkey from the pan, and using two forks, shred all the meat from the bones. You can discard the skin if you like but it crisps up pretty well.

Spread the turkey out on a baking sheet or in a roasting tray and pour over the jar of sauce (keep some back to serve, if you like), tossing the turkey around in it to fully coat it. Spread it in an even layer, then roast for 30–40 minutes, turning occasionally, so the meat become crispy.

Serve the turkey with pancakes, shredded cucumber and spring onions and the extra hoisin sauce, or with rice or noodles and steamed pak choi. It's also great in an Oriental-style salad.

# Ethiopian doro wat

This chicken stew is a popular Friday night dinner that survived the long journey from Ethiopia to Israel when the Israeli government helped move huge numbers of the Beta Israel community of Ethiopia to Israel around 20 years ago. It uses *berbere* — a warm and deep spice blend that is seen in many recipes from that part of Africa. I have included a recipe for it here, but it's actually pretty widely available online and in some supermarkets.

## Serves 4

### FOR THE BERBERE
3 tbsp hot paprika
3 tbsp cayenne pepper
1 tsp ground ginger
½ tsp ground cumin
½ tsp ground coriander
½ tsp ground black pepper
¾ tsp ground cardamom or the seeds
 from 5 pods
¼ tsp ground allspice
¼ tsp ground turmeric
¼ tsp ground cinnamon
¼ tsp ground cloves
¼ tsp ground nutmeg

### FOR THE STEW
4 tbsp olive oil
4 red onions, chopped
6 garlic cloves
5cm piece of fresh ginger, peeled and grated
2 tbsp berbere spice blend
4 bone-in chicken thighs and 4 chicken legs
salt and freshly ground black pepper
250ml chicken stock (from a cube is fine)
250g passata
4 hard-boiled eggs

Mix all the ingredients for the berbere spice blend together and store in an airtight container until needed.

Heat the olive oil in a heavy-based pan or casserole dish. Add the onions and cook over a medium heat for about 10 minutes, stirring often, then add the garlic, ginger and the berbere. Cook, stirring, for about 2 minutes.

Add the chicken pieces and stir them around, coating them with the onions and spices. Season well with salt and pepper then add the chicken stock and passata. Bring to the boil, then lower the heat, cover with a lid and simmer for about 1 hour, until the chicken is tender, adding more stock if it seems to be drying out.

Remove the shells from the eggs and prick them a few times with a fork or skewer. Add to the stew and heat through.

Serve with flatbreads and a tomato, red onion and coriander salad, if you like.

# Chicken livers & onions in pita with tahini

The Jerusalem Mixed Grill is one of Israel's favourite street foods. Cooked on a flat grill (so essentially fried) it consists of a mixture of spiced chicken livers, heart and spleen, scooped into pita with fried onions, mango pickle (known as *amba* – you can find this in Middle Eastern grocers and Indian shops – it is savoury, more like lime pickle than mango chutney) and tahini. It is literally worth the trip to the Mahane Yehuda market in Jerusalem just to try it, but assuming you can't go there right now, and spleen isn't widely stocked by your butcher, here's a version with chicken livers, chicken breast and onions. Try it. It's ridiculously good.

**Serves 4**

2 tbsp olive oil
1 large onion, sliced
1 tsp ground turmeric
½ tsp ground coriander
½ tsp ground cumin
1 chicken breast, cut into cubes
500g chicken livers, trimmed of any
    sinew and cut into bite-sized pieces
2 garlic cloves, crushed
a pinch of ground allspice
a good grating of nutmeg
½ tsp salt
a good grinding of black pepper
4 pita breads, to serve
4 tsp mango pickle (*amba*)
1 tbsp tahini mixed with 100ml water
    and a pinch of salt
coriander leaves, to garnish

Heat the olive oil in a large, non-stick frying pan. Add the onion and cook over a medium heat for 5 minutes, until it starts to soften and turn golden brown.

Add the turmeric, coriander and cumin and cook, stirring, for 2–3 minutes, then turn up the heat and add the chicken breast and livers – you want some charred bits so keep the heat high and don't overcrowd the pan. You might need to do this in two batches.

Add the garlic, allspice, nutmeg, salt and pepper and cook for another few minutes, then taste and season with more salt and pepper if necessary.

Cut a slit in each pita bread to make a pocket then pile in the meat, top with a spoonful of mango pickle and drizzle with the tahini sauce. Sprinkle with coriander leaves and enjoy.

# Duck, fig & pomegranate New Year salad

At Rosh Hashanah, the Jewish New Year, it is traditional to eat foods that are sweet. This fits the bill perfectly – duck is so good with sweet accompaniments that it doesn't feel forced or sickly. It's also such an elegant dish it can be served to guests (halve the quantities for a starter) or as a grown-up treat supper when the kids are in bed, with a decent bottle of Shiraz, which is how I most enjoy it. This whole dish takes about 15 minutes to make and if you want to prep it in advance you can sear and crisp the duck breasts and make the sauce and salad ahead. Then all you have to do is pop the duck and figs in the oven and reheat the sauce before serving.

## Serves 4

4 duck breasts (about 750g in total)
salt and freshly ground black pepper
1 star anise
1 garlic clove, unpeeled
2 thyme sprigs
8 figs, quartered
100ml Marsala or Kiddush wine
2 tbsp red wine vinegar
2 tbsp orange juice
100g hazelnuts
200g baby spinach leaves
100g rocket leaves
1 red onion, thinly sliced
100g pomegranate seeds

Preheat the oven to 180°C/Gas 4.

Score the skin of the duck breasts in a criss-cross pattern with a sharp knife and then season all over with salt and pepper.

Put the duck breasts in a cold frying pan, skin-side down, with the star anise, garlic clove and thyme sprigs. Turn on the heat and cook over a medium heat until the skin crisps up. You will need to pour off the fat from time to time, as it melts away. Keep going until the thick layer of fat under the skin has all but disappeared. This will take about 6 minutes.

When the skin is nice and crisp and the fat has rendered away, turn the breasts over to sear them on the bottom, then place in a roasting dish with the star anise, garlic and thyme. (If you want, you can cool them down and place them in the fridge at this stage. Just bring them up to room temperature by taking them out of the fridge about 30 minutes before you are ready to finish the dish.)

When you are ready, add the quartered figs to the roasting dish and place in the oven for 8–10 minutes only – you want the duck pink in the middle so set a timer and keep an eye on it! When the duck breasts are ready, set the pan aside, covered with foil, for the duck to rest.

Remove any remaining fat from the frying pan, then pour in the wine, turn up the heat, and scrape any lovely tasty crispy bits from the bottom of the pan – they will become part of your dressing. Bubble until the wine has reduced by half, then add the vinegar and orange juice and keep bubbling until you have a glossy sauce. Taste it – there shouldn't be a flavour of alcohol and it shouldn't be too sweet. If either is the case, reduce a bit further. Season with salt and pepper and set aside. (If you want, you can make the sauce in advance too and just reheat it to serve it.)

Meanwhile, put the hazelnuts in a small roasting dish and roast them for 5 minutes. Remove and roughly smash them up with a rolling pin or in a pestle and mortar.

To assemble the salad, place the spinach and rocket leaves on a platter. Top with the red onion and hazelnuts. Slice the duck breasts on the diagonal into about five pieces. Arrange with the figs on top of the leaves.

Pour any juices from the roasting dish into the sauce and check the seasoning again. Pour the sauce over the duck and sprinkle with the pomegranate seeds. Serve immediately.

# Meat

# Salt beef

I know brining your own beef to make salt beef from scratch is very on-trend, but you can buy it ready-pickled in so many places now and frankly, although I love pickling, the idea of having a piece of beef submerged in brine in my garage, needing turning every day for over a week, simply doesn't appeal. However, cooking a piece of pickled beef for a couple of hours and serving it with rye bread, pickles, coleslaw, latkes (see page 174) and mustard or piccalilli (see page 196), definitely appeals! Here's how to do it. . .

**Serves 4**

1.6kg flat piece of pickled beef brisket
   (this is available in many supermarkets
   and from butchers)
2 bay leaves
2 onions, peeled and halved
6 carrots, peeled but left whole
1 tsp black peppercorns
4 allspice berries

Put the pickled beef into a large pan with all the other ingredients and cover with cold water. Bring to the boil, skimming away any scum that rises to the surface.

Reduce the heat, cover and simmer gently for 2½–3½ hours, or until a fork pushed into the meat slides in easily – it should be really soft.

Lift the meat onto a board and slice it into fairly thick slices.

Serve hot or cold, with whatever accompaniments you prefer (see above).

# Slow-cooked brisket in Kiddush wine

Apologies in advance, Mum, but when I was growing up, I used to dread having braised meat for dinner – thin slices of brown meat, swimming in watery gravy with slices of carrot and celery. These days, however, slow-cooked brisket couldn't be more in fashion – but with the meat caramelised first, before being cooked in a rich, onion gravy. It took me some time to perfect it but I found the key in a bottle of Kiddush wine – the sweet wine used to bring in the Sabbath on a Friday night with candles and challah. If you don't have a bottle, use port or any other sweet red wine.

**Serves 4**

1.4kg flat (not rolled) piece of beef brisket
2 tsp sweet paprika
1 tsp salt
½ tsp freshly ground black pepper
2 tbsp sunflower oil
600g shallots, halved lengthways
1 whole bulb of garlic, halved across
    the middle
350ml Palwins Kiddush wine (or use port
    or another sweet red wine)
1 beef stock cube, diluted in 350ml
    boiling water
1 star anise

Preheat the oven to 170°C/Gas 3.

Rub the brisket all over with the paprika, salt and pepper. Heat half the oil in a frying pan and brown the meat all over. You want it really caramelised so be patient and get a really good colour on each side before turning it over. Place the browned meat in a roasting tin or large casserole dish.

Add the remaining oil to the frying pan and cook the shallots over a low-medium heat. You want to get them really meltingly soft so, again, patience is key (it will take around 20 minutes). When they are golden and soft, tip them over and around the meat. Fry the garlic bulb halves, cut-side down, briefly in the same pan, just to get a little colour on them, then add them to the meat.

Now pour the wine or port into the pan and turn up the heat, scraping the bottom of the frying pan to get any caramelised bits, then pour it over the meat and onions. Add the beef stock and the star anise. Cover with a double layer of foil, tucked properly around so it's really well sealed, or with a lid if you are using a casserole dish. Cook in the oven for 2½ hours, checking every so often that it isn't drying out and topping up with more stock or water if necessary, then remove the foil or lid and cook for a further 20 minutes.

Remove the brisket and set aside, covered, to rest. Discard the star anise and papery garlic skins, and bubble the gravy on the hob, either in the tin or transferred to a small pan, until it reduces to a thicker, glossy sauce. Taste and season with more salt and pepper, if necessary. Slice the brisket and serve with mash and the onion gravy spooned on top.

# Stuffed cabbage leaves

At home, when I was growing up, these were a real treat. We called them by their Yiddish name, *holishkes*, and to me they are still the ultimate in comfort food – cabbage leaves with a succulent mince filling, in a sweet and sour tomato sauce. There many variations: Middle Eastern versions have dill and mint in them and sometimes currants; Hungarian rolls are made with marjoram; Polish ones are really sweet; some have rice, others don't; some are lamb, others are beef. These are my favourite. Their precise origin? My mum's kitchen.

**Serves 4**

FOR THE CABBAGE PARCELS
1 large white cabbage
500g minced meat (I like a mixture of beef and chicken)
1 onion, finely chopped
2 garlic cloves, crushed
1 potato, peeled and coarsely grated
1 egg
1 tbsp finely chopped thyme
1 tbsp finely chopped flat-leaf parsley
½ tsp hot paprika
a pinch of ground cinnamon
salt and freshly ground black pepper

FOR THE TOMATO SAUCE
500g passata
200ml water
2 tbsp tomato purée
3 tbsp lemon juice
2 tbsp soft light brown sugar
salt and freshly ground black pepper

First, put the whole cabbage in a large pan of water. Bring to the boil and simmer for 5 minutes, then remove the cabbage. You want the leaves to be pliable but not fully cooked.

Meanwhile, mix the remaining ingredients for the parcels in a bowl until well combined. Season generously and set aside.

Place all the sauce ingredients into a pan and put over a low heat to start simmering while you make the parcels.

Carefully remove the outer cabbage leaves – you will need about 12 decent-sized leaves but go for as many as you can. Finely shred the remaining cabbage, discarding the tough core, and add it to the simmering sauce.

Take the larger leaves and, for any that have a very thick stem, carefully 'shave' away some of the stem with a small, sharp knife, without cutting through the leaf itself, to make it thinner and more pliable.

Put about 1–2 tablespoons of the filling mixture (depending on the size of each leaf) in a sausage shape in the middle of the leaf. Roll it up, tucking in the sides as you go. Place the completed parcels in a deep frying pan, pushing them next to each other so they hold each other together.

Taste the tomato sauce. It might need more lemon juice, sugar, salt or pepper – or all four! Pour the sauce over the stuffed cabbage leaves. Simmer, covered, for around 1 hour, then remove the lid and summer for a further 15 minutes. Leave to cool slightly, for 10 minutes or so, before serving with rice or boiled potatoes.

# Beef tzimmes with carrots & prunes

Just the thought of eating meltingly sweet carrots with a savoury, pillowy dumpling, immediately transports me to my grandma's house as a child. I have never managed to replicate her version exactly but this is a pretty good variation with prunes and pieces of beef — turning it from a side dish to a main meal. I learnt recently that *tzimmes* is traditionally served at Jewish New Year because its sweetness is supposed to be a good omen for the year ahead, but I don't remember us eating it then — I think we just had it when Grandma happened to fancy making it!

**Serves 4**

1kg stewing beef, cut into cubes
salt and freshly ground black pepper
2 tbsp sunflower oil
1 large onion, cut into eighths
8 large carrots, cut on the diagonal
    into large chunks
300g pitted prunes
2 tbsp honey
2 tbsp lemon juice
2 tbsp soft dark brown sugar
1 tsp ground cinnamon
1 tsp ground ginger
grated zest and juice of 1 orange
750ml beef stock (from a cube is fine)

FOR THE DUMPLINGS
225g medium matzah meal
a pinch of ground ginger
a pinch of ground cinnamon
2 tbsp margarine or chicken fat
salt and freshly ground black pepper
2 eggs, beaten
about 100ml hot water

Preheat the oven to 170°C/Gas 3.

First, make the dumplings. Rub the matzah meal, ginger, cinnamon and fat together in a bowl as if you were making pastry. Season with salt and pepper. Add the beaten eggs and enough hot water (about 100ml) to bring the mixture together, then put it in the fridge while you prepare everything else.

Season the meat with salt and pepper. Heat half the sunflower oil in a frying pan and sear the beef cubes until they are browned on all sides. Place in a roasting dish.

Place the onion, carrots, prunes, honey, lemon juice and brown sugar in a large bowl and sprinkle over the cinnamon, ginger, orange zest and some salt and pepper. Pour over the remaining oil and the orange juice and toss to combine. Tip into the roasting dish and spread out evenly around the meat.

Now make the dumplings by rolling the matzah meal mixture into small balls, around the size of a walnut. Scatter among the other ingredients in the dish and pour over the beef stock.

Cover the dish tightly with foil and place in the oven. Cook for 1½ hours, checking the liquid levels a couple of times during cooking and topping up if necessary. You want the dumplings to have absorbed most of the liquid, leaving a sweet, shiny film on the carrots.

# Lamb in coriander sauce from Cochin

This is another recipe adapted from the amazing Indian Jewish cookery book *Spice & Kosher: Exotic Cuisine of the Cochin Jews.* It has a ton of ingredients but is really easy to make and beautifully fragrant and mild – but if you are one of those people with a genetic propensity to hate coriander, look away now!

**Serves 4**

2 tbsp coconut oil or sunflower oil

500g cubed lamb shoulder

2 onions, chopped

a large bunch of coriander leaves, chopped

1 mild green chilli, deseeded and finely chopped

2 garlic cloves, very finely chopped

5cm piece of fresh ginger, peeled and grated

2 tbsp ground coriander

1 tsp ground turmeric

½ tsp fennel seeds

seeds from 2 cardamom pods

a pinch of ground cloves

a pinch of ground cinnamon

2 tsp mild chilli powder

4 curry leaves

1 tomato, chopped

a good pinch of salt

200ml water

2 tbsp toasted flaked almonds, to garnish (*optional*)

Heat the oil in a large pan or deep-sided frying pan over a medium heat. Add the lamb cubes and fry until the lamb is brown on all sides, then add the onion and fry until softened, about 10 minutes.

Add the chopped coriander, chilli, garlic and ginger and cook for a further 2 minutes. Add the remaining spices, the curry leaves, chopped tomato and salt and cook for a further 2–3 minutes, stirring occasionally.

Add the water and bring to the boil, then reduce the heat and simmer very gently for 1 hour, uncovered. Keep an eye on it and add a little more water if it dries out.

Garnish with toasted flaked almonds, if using, and serve with rice.

# Roman braised lamb shoulder with cloves, cinnamon & olives

This recipe is adapted from one in *Cucina Ebraica: Flavors of the Italian Jewish Kitchen* by Joyce Goldstein, which I cook from often. This recipe is so simple yet tastes very special and the cloves, cinnamon and orange zest make it summery and exotic.

**Serves 4**

1.2kg cubed lamb shoulder
a pinch of ground cloves
½ tsp ground cinnamon
salt and freshly ground black pepper
2 tbsp olive oil
3 onions, sliced
2 garlic cloves, thinly sliced
150ml white wine
500ml chicken stock (from a cube is fine)
1 tbsp chopped fresh rosemary
1 tbsp chopped fresh thyme
1 bay leaf
grated zest of 1 orange
4 sweet potatoes, peeled and cut into
    chunks about the same size as the lamb
about 20 pitted green olives (the ones that
    come in the sachets with herbs are good)

Place the lamb in a bowl and season it with the cloves, cinnamon and salt and pepper. Heat about half the oil in a frying pan over a medium heat and brown the cubes of meat on all sides, in batches, transferring them to a heavy-based pan as you go.

Add the onions to the frying pan, with a little more oil if necessary, and cook until softened and translucent, about 10 minutes. Add the garlic and cook for a further minute, then add to the lamb in the pan.

Add the white wine to the frying pan and turn up the heat, scraping the bottom of the pan to deglaze it. Pour the wine mixture over the lamb and onions and add enough stock to just cover the meat. Cover and simmer gently for 1 hour, then add the chopped herbs, bay leaf, orange zest, sweet potatoes and olives. Cook for a further 30 minutes, covered, adding more stock if necessary.

Taste and adjust the seasoning before serving. I like this with steamed cavolo nero, which seems to suit its Italian origins. It is also fantastic with couscous.

# Lamb shanks with apricots

When we go to Israel on holiday, one of the highlights is to stay in a hotel for the weekend with the part of our family that lives there. The hotels always make extraordinary Friday night buffet dinners to welcome in the Sabbath, held in huge, noisy dining rooms full of jolly groups of families and friends. This delicately spiced lamb dish is based on something I tried at one of those buffets in a hotel called The Daniel in Herzilya, a coastal town where we have had many a happy Friday night supper at which my daughters and their Israeli cousins have been reunited after months of not seeing each other.

If you can't get hold of shanks, use a bone-in shoulder of lamb for this, but whatever you do, try it – and serve with hugs, laughter and lots of noise!

## Serves 4

2 tbsp plain flour
¼ tsp ground cinnamon
¼ tsp ground ginger
¼ tsp ground cloves
½ tsp ground cumin
½ tsp ground coriander
1 tsp ground turmeric
1 tsp hot paprika
salt and freshly ground black pepper
4 lamb shanks, each weighing about 400–500g
2 tbsp olive oil
12 shallots
3 garlic cloves, crushed
2 celery sticks, chopped
4 carrots, sliced
1 bay leaf
1 thyme sprig
500ml chicken stock (from a cube is fine)
20 dried apricots

Preheat the oven to 170°C/Gas 3.

Put the flour in a large plastic sandwich-type bag with all the ground spices and a generous pinch of salt and plenty of black pepper. Add the lamb shanks and shake them around, making sure they are fully coated with the mixture.

Heat the olive oil in a frying pan over a medium heat and have a casserole dish at the ready. Brown the lamb shanks on all sides, being careful not to burn them. Place the browned lamb shanks in the casserole dish and add all the other ingredients – including any remaining flour and spice mix and any bits from the bottom of the frying pan (you can deglaze the pan with a little of the stock, if you like).

Put the lid on the dish, place in the oven and cook for 3 hours, then remove the lid and cook for a further 30 minutes, by which time the meat should be falling off the bone.

Skim off any fat from the top of the dish and discard. Serve the lamb shanks with rice or couscous.

# Lamb & hummus pita pockets

There is a little place hidden around the back of the Carmel Market in Tel Aviv called M25 that is a butcher shop and restaurant specialising in meat. One of their most popular dishes is Lebanese-style *arayes* – pita bread that is halved, spread with tahini, filled with seasoned lamb mince, fried in beef fat, then crisped in the oven. Here's my adaptation – I used hummus rather than tahini when I tried it out at home purely because I had some in the fridge and it was so good I have kept it in there.

**Serves 4**

600g lamb mince
salt and freshly ground black pepper
a small bunch of flat-leaf parsley, chopped
4 large round pitas, ideally from a Middle Eastern grocery as these tend to hold together better than the supermarket ones (or use 8 smaller ones and give everyone 2 each)
4 generous tbsp hummus (see page 184)
1 tbsp olive oil
extra hummus and hot sauce, to serve

Preheat the oven to 180°C/Gas 4.

Place a frying pan over a medium-high heat and add the lamb mince. Fry it, breaking it up with a fork or wooden spoon as you go. You shouldn't need any extra oil as the mince will have enough fat to stop it sticking. Season well with salt and pepper and cook for a few minutes, until the lamb is cooked through but still tender. Add the parsley and stir through.

Halve the pitas and carefully scoop out and discard any extra doughy bread in the middle. Spread the inside of each pita pocket with hummus, then fill with the lamb mince.

Heat the olive oil in a clean frying pan. Fry the filled pita halves on each side until crisp. (You can now set aside the pitas until you are ready to serve them or finish them straight away.)

Put the filled pitas on a baking tray and bake in the oven for 15 minutes, turning them halfway through cooking.

Cut the crisp pita breads into halves and serve with some extra hummus and hot sauce on the side, if you wish.

# Middle Eastern meat pie

This is based on something I ate in Tel Aviv Port at a restaurant called Meat and Eat; it was so clever, I had to steal the idea. It is not only insanely good, it's also really easy to make and such a crowd-pleaser – I'm pretty excited to share it with you! If you have an ovenproof frying pan, you can simply put the pastry lid on it and put the whole thing in the oven, which is how it was served in the restaurant and looks pretty cool. I transferred it to a pie dish – either way does it for me!

**Serves 4**

2 tbsp olive oil
1 onion, chopped
1 aubergine, diced
1 garlic clove, chopped
500g lamb mince
¼ tsp ground cinnamon
½ tsp ground coriander
½ tsp ground cumin
1 rosemary sprig, leaves picked and finely chopped
2 tbsp tomato purée
a splash of Worcestershire sauce
100ml red wine
1 x 400g tin of chickpeas, rinsed and drained
a small bunch of flat-leaf parsley, chopped
salt and freshly ground black pepper
1 x 320g sheet of puff pastry
2 tbsp hummus
1 egg, beaten

Preheat the oven to 220°C/Gas 7.

Heat the oil in a large frying pan and add the onion and aubergine. Cook over a medium heat, stirring occasionally, until the onion is soft and translucent.

Add the garlic and cook for a further minute, then add the lamb and cook it for about 10 minutes, breaking up the mince as you stir it, to brown it all over.

Add the cinnamon, coriander, cumin and rosemary and stir well, then add the tomato purée, Worcestershire sauce and red wine. Bring to the boil and let it bubble until the liquid has reduced by half, about 5 minutes. Now add the chickpeas and parsley, season really well and, if you are not using an ovenproof frying pan, tip it all into a pie dish (I use a 26cm rectangular enamel pie dish). If you are using a frying pan, let it cool down before you move to the next stage.

Roll out your pastry to fit whatever dish you are using. Leaving a 2cm border all around the edge, spread the pastry generously with the hummus.

Brush beaten egg around the rim of your pie dish or around the edge of your frying pan. Place the pastry, hummus-side down, over the filling. Seal carefully around the edges by pressing with your fingers. Brush the top of the pastry with more beaten egg and cut 3 slits in the centre with a sharp knife to allow steam to escape as it cooks.

Bake for 30 minutes, or until the pastry is well risen and golden brown. Serve immediately.

# Stuffed artichoke bottoms

It was a revelation to me when I first realised that frozen or jarred artichoke bottoms are not only readily available, but are also pretty cheap! Since then I have used them in all sorts of recipes — I sometimes simply cook them with broad beans, mint, lemon juice and olive oil, or I love them stuffed with rice or meat. Here I've stuffed them with lamb mince — although you are welcome to use beef — and cooked them in a tomato sauce.

**Serves 4**

8 frozen artichoke bottoms (or from a jar)
500g lamb or beef mince
1 garlic clove, crushed
1 tbsp tomato purée
a small bunch of flat-leaf parsley,
    finely chopped
a few mint leaves, finely chopped
a few dill fronds, finely chopped
salt and freshly ground black pepper
500g passata
1 tsp sugar

Preheat the oven to 180°C/Gas 4 and find a roasting dish that will hold your artichoke bottoms snugly.

If using frozen artichokes, leave them to defrost. If using jarred, drain them well.

To make the filling, mix together the lamb or beef mince, garlic, tomato purée, half of the parsley and most of the mint and dill, leaving a little for garnish. Season really well.

Fill the artichoke bottoms with the stuffing mixture, mounding it up slightly. Pour the jar of passata into your roasting dish. Half-fill the empty jar with water, swirl it around to get all the passata out and add that too. Add the sugar and a teaspoon of salt and stir together in the dish, then place the filled artichoke bottoms in the sauce, arranging them snugly.

Bake in the oven for 45 minutes. Sprinkle with the remaining fresh herbs and serve with rice, if you like.

# Pulled lamb

For the last few years we have held a summer party at our house for old friends – many of whom my husband Dan and I have known since we were teenagers and now have kids of their own, who are friends with our kids. It's always fun with bunting and a bouncy castle and LOTS of meat! This is one of the success stories from last year. A shoulder of lamb, cooked low and slow with a barbecue rub, and slathered with barbecue sauce for the last 30 minutes of cooking. This also works really well with whole turkey thighs or with brisket, and the sauce and rub are also great on ribs. Just add buns or wraps, pickles and slaw. And good friends, of course.

**Serves 4–6**

1.5kg shoulder of lamb on the bone

FOR THE RUB
1 tbsp hot paprika
1 tbsp soft dark brown sugar
1 tsp cayenne pepper
1 tsp chipotle flakes
1 tsp dried oregano
1 tsp garlic powder
1 tsp salt
1 tsp ground black pepper

FOR THE BARBECUE SAUCE
4 tbsp tomato purée
2 tbsp cider or red wine vinegar
2 tbsp maple syrup
2 tbsp pomegranate molasses
2 tbsp soy sauce
1 tsp chipotle flakes
salt and freshly ground black pepper

Preheat the oven to 150°C/Gas 2.

Mix all the rub ingredients together in a small bowl and set aside. In a separate bowl, mix all the sauce ingredients together and set aside.

Massage the rub into the lamb, making sure you get it into all the crevices. Now place the lamb in a roasting tray, add a cup of water and cover it really well with foil, sealing it in completely. Cook in the oven for 4 hours, or until the meat is so tender it is falling apart.

Remove the foil and pour the barbecue sauce over the lamb. Increase the oven temperature to 180°C/Gas 4 and cook for a further 30 minutes before serving. Transfer to a large plate and pull the meat apart with two forks into bite-sized pieces, discarding any fatty parts. Skim off any fat from the pan and pour the juices over the top. Serve with good-quality burger buns or wraps to pile it into, green salad, coleslaw and pickles.

# Vegetarian
# Dishes

# Shakshuka

Shakshuka is one of my favourite meals — and words — in the world. It means 'mixed up' or 'shaken up', depending on where you believe the word originated; variants are eaten all over the Middle East, though it is apparently originally Libyan. In Israel it can be eaten for breakfast, brunch, lunch or even supper and aside from the three main ingredients — eggs, tomatoes and chilli — it's a real open book as to what you can add. I've had it with sausages, feta, aubergine, fennel, leeks, red peppers, spinach, kale. . . and that means you can make it with whatever you happen to have in your fridge. So here's my favourite version — but feel free to mix it up!

You will need a large, deep frying pan, with a lid, ideally with a hole in it or a valve to let out the steam. Purists insist on cooking the eggs in the oven but the hob works perfectly well for me. They also like to use fresh tomatoes, but mine come out of a tin.

**Serves 2**

2 tbsp olive oil
1 large onion, chopped
2 garlic cloves, crushed
1 red chilli, finely chopped (deseed if
   you prefer less heat)
1 tsp smoked paprika
½ tsp ground cumin
1 x 400g tin of tomatoes
1 tbsp tomato purée
salt and freshly ground black pepper
2 handfuls of baby spinach leaves
4 eggs
75g feta, drained and crumbled
chopped coriander, to serve

Heat the oil in a deep frying pan. Add the onion and cook over a low-medium heat for 10 minutes until soft and translucent. Add the garlic, chilli, paprika and cumin and cook for a further 3 minutes.

Pour in the tin of tomatoes and add the tomato purée. Season well with salt and pepper and then allow to simmer gently for 5 minutes.

Add the spinach leaves by gently stirring them into the sauce — they will wilt almost immediately.

Make four hollows in the sauce with the back of a spoon and crack an egg into each one. Sprinkle over the feta and cover with a lid. Leave to cook over a medium heat for 5 minutes, or until the whites of the eggs are set.

Serve with crusty bread and garnish with chopped coriander.

# Matza brei

When I was little, *matza brei* — which is essentially eggs scrambled with matza crackers — meant it was Passover, the Jewish festival when no bread or 'leavened' product is allowed to be eaten. For breakfast, for a whole week, it was *matza brei* every day — and I loved it. It was only when I was older that I realised how many variations there are of this dish. In my house it was always savoury but other recipes suggest it should be sprinkled with sugar or served with apple sauce and sour cream or even — god forbid — jam! It can also look like a frittata or an omelette but this is the way I had it and the way I serve it to my daughters. The only tradition I have broken is that I make it all year round — it's too good to save for Passover!

**Serves 2**

4 matzah sheets
4 eggs, beaten
salt and freshly ground black pepper
1 tbsp sunflower oil

Fill a bowl with warm water. Crush the matzah into the water into pieces roughly the size of a postage stamp. Leave them for 1 minute, then drain the water away, pressing the matzah against the side of the bowl to squeeze out the liquid.

Pour the eggs over the matzah and season well with salt and pepper. Mix well to combine.

Heat the oil in a frying pan over a medium heat. Pour in the egg-soaked matzah and cook for about 5 minutes, stirring, until the eggs are cooked and the matzah has turned crisp in some places. Serve immediately.

# Syrian courgette & cheese pies

These soft, pillowy little open pies, called *fatayer,* are popular all over the Middle East where they are often grabbed as a snack from a market stall, served on platters at parties or served for lunch with a mound of tomato and cucumber salad. Shaped like petals, or boats, they couldn't be prettier and you can experiment with all sorts of fillings – meat and spinach are traditional. The dough only takes about 20 minutes to rise so you can make the filling during that time and have them on the table shortly after.

**Makes 16–24 depending on size**

FOR THE DOUGH
350g plain flour
7g sachet instant yeast
2 tsp granulated sugar
½ tsp salt
200ml lukewarm milk or water
75ml olive oil, plus extra for oiling and brushing

FOR THE FILLING
3 courgettes, coarsely grated
200g feta, drained and crumbled
1 tbsp sumac
a small bunch of flat-leaf parsley, chopped
1 egg, beaten
salt and freshly ground black pepper

Mix together the flour, yeast, sugar and salt in a bowl. Add the milk or water and olive oil. Knead by hand or in a free-standing mixer fitted with a dough hook until the dough is soft and no longer sticky. Coat a bowl with a little olive oil, form the dough into a neat ball and place in the bowl. Cover with lightly greased cling film and leave to rise somewhere warm until it doubles in size, about 20 minutes.

Preheat the oven to 200°C/Gas 6.

Meanwhile, place the grated courgettes in a colander to drain over a sink. When you are ready to make the filling, squeeze them with a clean tea towel to remove as much moisture as possible. Add the squeezed courgette to a bowl with the other filling ingredients and mix gently to combine.

Form the dough into 16 balls (or 24 smaller balls) and roll each ball into a long oval shape about 5mm thick. Place around 1–2 tablespoons of filling in the centre of each oval.

Fold one long edge a little bit over the filling, forming a frame for it but leaving some filling exposed. Press down to seal at each end of the folded edge. Do the same on the other side, forming a petal or boat shape. Pinch the edges well to seal. Repeat with the remaining dough pieces and place them on lightly oiled baking sheets. (You need to work quickly as the dough will continue to rise and the pies may open so you may want to bake one tray while finishing the second tray.)

Brush the edges with olive oil, then bake for about 15 minutes until the dough has turned golden brown and the cheese mixture has melted. Serve warm or at room temperature.

# Courgette & feta fritters with labneh & chilli relish

Versions of these little fritters pop up all over the Middle East and I regularly serve them when people come round for a glass of wine. They are delicious served with labneh (a very basic strained-yoghurt cheese) and a homemade chilli relish, both of which you'll need to prepare ahead of the fritters (although I often serve them with Greek yoghurt and shop-bought sweet chilli sauce if I am feeling lazy!). Do try making labneh one day – it is so easy and satisfying and you can pimp it up with herbs, garlic, chopped olives or whatever you like to make your own flavoured cheese spreads.

## Makes 16

3 courgettes, grated, as much liquid
   as possible squeezed out
100g self-raising flour
50g mature Cheddar, grated
100g feta, drained and crumbled
3 spring onions, finely chopped
2 eggs, beaten
1 tsp sumac
1 tsp nigella seeds
a handful of mint leaves, finely chopped
a few dill fronds, finely chopped
salt and freshly ground black pepper
sunflower oil (or other flavourless oil),
   for frying

FOR THE LABNEH
1kg full-fat natural yoghurt (not Greek)
½ tsp salt

FOR THE CHILLI RELISH
(MAKES 4 SMALL JARS)
20 red chillies
50g piece of fresh ginger, peeled
   and roughly chopped
10 garlic cloves
2 onions, roughly chopped
2 red peppers, deseeded and roughly
   chopped
1 x 400g tin of chopped tomatoes
250ml red wine vinegar
1 tbsp salt
1kg caster sugar

To make your own labneh mix the yoghurt with the salt and then dollop it into the middle of a cheesecloth or muslin or a clean J-cloth. Bring the four corners together and tie them at the top to make a Dick Whittington-style parcel. Put a wooden spoon handle through the knot and suspend the parcel over a bowl. Place in the fridge for 14–72 hours; after 14 hours you will have a thick, Greek yoghurt-style labneh dip – perfect for your fritters. After 2 days you will have a soft cheese, ideal for spreading. After 72 hours you will have a drier cheese that you can roll into balls, coat with chopped herbs or paprika and store in a jar, topped with olive oil, for a month in the fridge.

For the chilli relish: pulse the chillies, ginger, garlic, onions and peppers in a food processor until finely chopped. Place in a pan with the tomatoes, vinegar, salt and sugar. Bring slowly to the boil, then reduce the heat and simmer for 1 hour, until glossy and sticky – keep an eye on it so it doesn't burn. Cool slightly, then transfer to sterilised jars (I run mine through the dishwasher to sterilise them). These will keep, unopened, for up to 6 months. Store opened jars in the fridge for 2 weeks.

Mix all the ingredients for the fritters together in a large bowl and put in the fridge to firm up for 5 minutes.

Meanwhile, pour the oil into a large, high-sided frying pan to a depth of 3cm. Heat over a medium-high heat until a cube of bread dropped into the oil sizzles and turns golden in 30 seconds. Have ready a plate lined with kitchen paper.

Carefully drop tablespoons of the fritter mixture into the oil (cook in batches to avoid overcrowding the pan). Cook for 2 minutes on each side, or until really crisp on the outside. Drain on kitchen paper and sprinkle with a little salt. Serve hot or warm with the labneh and chilli relish for dipping.

# Roasted vegetable ratatouille

This is so far away from the sludgy, miserable ratatouille I remember from the seventies; it's a total revelation! This is a real celebration of the Mediterranean — and so easy to make. It is a great side dish with fish or chicken and delicious as a main course served with rice or couscous, topped with feta, if you like. You'll need a few baking trays for this one.

**Serves 4**

2 aubergines, cut into bite-sized chunks
3 courgettes, cut into bite-sized chunks
2 red peppers, deseeded and cut into into bite-sized chunks
2 red onions, cut into eighths
4 garlic cloves, unpeeled
200g button mushrooms
400g cherry tomatoes
1 fennel bulb, cut into bite-sized chunks (*optional*)
150ml olive oil
salt and freshly ground black pepper
a small bunch of basil, shredded

Preheat the oven to 200°C/Gas 6.

Put all the vegetables into a large bowl, toss with the olive oil and season with salt and pepper.

Spread out onto two or three baking sheets or in roasting dishes lined with baking parchment.

Roast in the oven for 40 minutes, or until the aubergines are golden brown and everything else is cooked. Transfer everything, including the juices, to a serving dish and toss with the shredded basil leaves. Taste and adjust the seasoning and then serve.

# Whole roasted cauliflower with fresh tomatoes & tahini sauce

You might be forgiven for thinking it was the Americans who started roasting cauliflowers all over the place and turning this previously pretty uninspiring vegetable into the food world's next big thing. But NO! It was the Israelis. Or one particular Israeli actually: a chef called Eyal Shani. At his business partner's house for Friday night dinner, he was served a whole roasted cauliflower — his partner's mother's recipe — and boom! It ended up on the restaurant menu as 'cauliflower three ways' and became an international sensation! This is such a dramatic and exciting dish to bring to the table — and so easy to make. It also works as a side dish, alongside a roast chicken, say.

**Serves 4 as a main, 8 as a side**

1 large cauliflower, most of the outer leaves removed but stem remaining
2 tbsp olive oil
1 tsp smoked sweet paprika
1 tsp paprika
2 tsp za'atar
salt and freshly ground black pepper
4 tomatoes

FOR THE TAHINI SAUCE
150g tahini
100ml cold water
1 garlic clove, crushed
juice of 1 lemon
salt and freshly ground black pepper

Preheat the oven to 180°C/Gas 4 and bring a large pan of water to the boil.

Carefully place the cauliflower into the water and let it cook for 8 minutes. Remove and place on a baking tray.

Mix the olive oil with the smoked paprika, paprika and za'atar. Spread this mixture all over the cauliflower with the back of a spoon and then season with salt and pepper. Place in the oven for 45 minutes, until cooked through and crisp on the outside.

Meanwhile, skin the tomatoes. Cut a small cross in their base with a sharp knife, then plunge them into boiling water and then immediately into cold water. Remove the skins, which will have loosened. Grate the tomatoes with a coarse grater into a small bowl.

Mix the tahini with the water, garlic, lemon juice, salt and pepper, ideally in a food processor or in a bowl with a whisk.

Serve the cauliflower either in florets or cut into 'steaks' with the tahini sauce and grated tomato on top.

# Green pashtida

I insisted that my lovely friend and regular partner-in-eating Jane Conley gave me this recipe after she made it for lunch at her house one Sunday. It is essentially a crustless quiche or baked frittata, the likes of which have become popular in trendy Israeli cafés, where they are called *pashtida*. They come in every variety imaginable — the recipe for *almodrote* that follows this one on page 151 is a similar egg, vegetable and cheese baked concoction.

**Serves 6**

1 tbsp olive oil, plus extra for greasing
6 spring onions, finely chopped
   (including the green ends)
2 leeks, finely chopped
150g broccoli, broken into small florets
100g fine asparagus
300g spinach
200g frozen peas
8 eggs
125g ricotta
300g mature Cheddar, grated
1 tsp baking powder
1 tsp English mustard
a good grating of nutmeg
salt and freshly ground black pepper

Preheat the oven to 190°C/Gas 5. Lightly grease a 30 x 20cm rectangular oven dish.

Heat the oil in a large frying pan. Add the spring onions and leeks and fry over a medium heat for 10 minutes, until softened.

Meanwhile, bring a large pan of water to the boil. Add the broccoli and cook for 3 minutes, then add the asparagus and cook for a further 2 minutes. Drain and rinse under cold water so they keep their bright green colour, then set aside.

Add the spinach and peas to the onions and leeks and stir until the spinach has wilted and the peas are defrosted. Turn off the heat and set aside.

Beat the eggs in a bowl and stir in the ricotta, Cheddar, baking powder, mustard, nutmeg and salt and pepper.

Tip all the vegetables into the greased oven dish. Pour over the egg mixture, then bake in the oven for 25 minutes, or until set and golden brown on top.

Allow to stand for 10 minutes before serving warm or at room temperature, with salad and bread.

# Sephardic aubergine & cheese almodrote

This recipe is based on a Turkish Sephardic dish from the brilliant Gil Marks's book *Olive Trees and Honey*. In the Ottoman Empire, Sephardic vegetable, egg and cheese concoctions were widely eaten and were known as *almodrote* or *almudroti*, which means 'hodgepodge'. You can replace the aubergines with roasted courgettes, if you prefer.

**Serves 4**

3 aubergines (about 600g)
2 garlic cloves, crushed
3 eggs, beaten
150g feta, drained and crumbled
150g mature Cheddar, grated,
    plus 50g for sprinkling
5 tbsp medium matzah meal or dried
    breadcrumbs, plus 1 tbsp for sprinkling
a pinch of sugar
1 tsp hot paprika
a small bunch of dill, finely chopped
salt and freshly ground black pepper
2 tbsp olive oil

Preheat the oven to 200°C/Gas 6 and lightly grease a shallow oven dish, about 17 x 28cm.

Place the aubergines on a baking sheet and roast them for about 45 minutes, until tender. Remove them from the oven and allow to cool until you can handle them. Keep the oven on but turn it down to 180°C/Gas 4.

Split the aubergines and, discarding the skins, carefully scoop out all the flesh, putting it in a sieve over a bowl so the liquid can drain out. Leave it to drain while you mix together all the other ingredients in a bowl, except the oil. Season with salt and pepper.

When the liquid has stopped dripping from the aubergine — after about 15 minutes — chop the aubergine into rough chunks and stir it into the rest of the mixture.

Pour the mixture into the oven dish and sprinkle with the extra matzah meal or breadcrumbs and the extra grated Cheddar. Finally, drizzle over the olive oil. Bake for 45 minutes, until set and golden. Let stand for at least 10 minutes before serving.

# Whole roasted aubergine with tahini, date syrup & pomegranate

The first time I cooked a whole aubergine this way I almost laughed out loud. It must be the easiest supper of all time. Just pop the aubergine in the oven, top it with lovely things and eat. Like a jacket potato, I guess, but much more exciting!

**Serves 1**

1 aubergine
1 tbsp good-quality extra-virgin olive oil
salt and freshly ground black pepper
about 2 tbsp tahini sauce (see page 144)
1 tbsp date syrup (*silan*)
a small handful of pomegranate seeds
a small handful of toasted pine nuts
a small bunch of flat-leaf parsley, chopped

Preheat the oven to 170°C/Gas 3.

Place the whole aubergine on a baking sheet and bake in the oven for 1 hour.

Take it out and, using tongs, put it on a plate. With a small, sharp knife, cut down the aubergine lengthways, keeping it joined at the top where the stem is. Slightly flatten the aubergine halves so they sit steadily on the plate.

Drizzle with the olive oil and season with salt and pepper. Next, drizzle over the tahini sauce, then the date syrup. Sprinkle over the pomegranate seeds and pine nuts and finish with plenty of chopped parsley. Eat immediately.

# The ultimate veggie burger

If you are ever in Tel Aviv, go to Hashomer 1, a little place right near the Carmel Market where you will want to eat EVERYTHING. I actually did, in the name of book research, of course, and one of the best things they do is 'veggie balls' in a sandwich with tahini, mango pickle (*amba*), fried aubergines, salad and hard-boiled eggs. This, I need to share with you, though I have made the balls into fritters — they fit into the sandwich more easily.

**Serves 4**

1 raw beetroot, grated
1 carrot, grated
1 courgette, grated
1 potato, grated
3 tbsp plain flour
salt and freshly ground black pepper
1 egg, beaten
sunflower oil (or other flavourless oil),
    for frying
1 aubergine, sliced into rounds
4 challah rolls or large brioche rolls
2 tbsp tahini or hummus
2 tbsp mango pickle (*amba*)
2 tomatoes, sliced
2 gherkins, sliced
2 hard-boiled eggs, sliced
4 little gem lettuce leaves

In a bowl, mix together the grated vegetables. Toss in the flour, season well, and mix in the egg.

Pour the sunflower oil into a deep frying pan, to a depth of 2cm. Heat until a cube of bread dropped into the oil sizzles and turns golden in 30 seconds. Gently drop spoonfuls of the mixture into it and fry over a medium heat for about 3 minutes on each side, until crisp. Remove and drain on kitchen paper, sprinkling with salt while they are still hot.

When they are cooked, season the aubergine slices and fry them, too, again transferring to kitchen paper to drain.

If you like, heat a griddle pan over a high heat and char the cut sides of the buns for a couple of minutes.

Spread one side of your bun with tahini (or hummus). Spread the other with mango pickle. Layer up the bun, putting the aubergine next to the tahini, then on top of it put a vegetable fritter, tomato slices, gherkin slices and egg slices, and top with a little gem lettuce leaf. Close the bun, with the mango pickle-spread half on top. Eat immediately.

# Salads
# & Sides

# Tomato, orange & mint salad

The combination of tomato and orange is unexpectedly pleasing and summery and will transport you to a sunny beachside café in a mouthful. This salad makes a fantastic accompaniment to anything just as it is but can be made more substantial with the addition of an avocado, 150g drained and crumbled feta and a handful of black olives.

## Serves 6

8 large, ripe tomatoes
100g cherry tomatoes
4 large oranges
1 tbsp maple syrup
1 tbsp lemon juice
2 tbsp extra-virgin olive oil
salt and freshly ground black pepper
a small handful of mint leaves,
    finely chopped

Using a serrated knife, cut the large ripe tomatoes in half and then each half into three segments. Place in a bowl. Halve the cherry tomatoes across the middle and add them, too.

Use a small, sharp knife to cut the ends off each orange, so you can stand them up on a board. Then cut vertically to slice away the peel and pith, following the contours of the fruit to keep it as spherical as possible. Cut out each segment, by cutting carefully alongside the membrane separating each segment. The orange segments will drop out, leaving the membrane behind. Add the orange segments to the tomato pieces.

Whisk together the maple syrup, lemon juice and olive oil. Pour it over the orange and tomato pieces. Season with salt and pepper and toss to combine.

Transfer to a serving dish and scatter with the finely chopped mint leaves.

# Peach, mozzarella & smoked salmon salad

This recipe came about because I saw a recipe for a peach and Parma ham salad and was looking for a way of recreating it without the ham. The smoked salmon has the same salty, smoky qualities and works really well. This is gorgeous served on a large platter but also works as a starter on individual plates – and is lovely even without the mozzarella, if you want to have a dairy-free version.

**Serves 6**

4 ripe peaches
250g mozzarella (2 large balls)
150g smoked salmon
a handful of fresh basil leaves
50g pomegranate seeds
50g toasted pine nuts (you can buy them toasted or simply heat in a small dry frying pan over a medium heat for a few minutes)

FOR THE DRESSING
2 tbsp pomegranate molasses
2 tbsp white wine vinegar
4 tbsp olive oil
salt and freshly ground black pepper

Cut the peaches in half, remove the stones and cut each half into four segments.

Arrange on a platter (or individual plates). Tear the mozzarella into bite-sized pieces and cut the smoked salmon into thin strips and arrange amongst the peach slices.

Scatter over the basil leaves, pomegranate seeds and pine nuts.

Whisk the dressing ingredients together and drizzle over the top. Serve immediately.

# Roasted carrots, fennel & onion with tahini & amba dressing

The dressing is the real star of the show here – *amba* is rather like the Marmite of condiments in Israel; some people really object to it, while others (like me) love it. It's not sweet like mango chutney, but instead is very sharp with a distinctive tang. Although I find it pretty addictive, it does need to be tempered with other flavours – the sweetness of the roasted vegetables and the savoury elements of the tahini work so well with it in this dish. You can pick it up easily in Middle Eastern grocers or Indian shops, or else you can buy a very similar Indian mango pickle in supermarkets.

**Serves 6**

450g baby carrots, scrubbed (or use regular carrots, peeled and cut lengthways into 4 long wedges)
2 large fennel bulbs, cut lengthways into 1cm slices, any fronds reserved
2 red onions, quartered
2 tbsp olive oil
salt and freshly ground black pepper
1 tbsp each of sesame and pumpkin seeds
1 tsp nigella seeds

FOR THE DRESSING
2 tbsp tahini
2 tbsp savoury mango pickle (*amba*)
    – not mango chutney
juice of 1 lemon
salt and freshly ground black pepper

Preheat the oven to 200°C/Gas 6.

Toss the vegetables in the olive oil and season well. Put them in a roasting tray and roast for 45 minutes, or until tender.

Meanwhile, for the dressing, mix the tahini with the mango pickle (discarding any large pieces of mango), the lemon juice and 4 tablespoons of cold water in a bowl. Season to taste.

Arrange the roasted vegetables on a platter. Drizzle over the dressing and scatter with the seeds. Serve at room temperature.

# Za'atar & garlic roasted tomatoes

We have had many happy holidays visiting my husband's family, who are British but now live in Israel. For me, one of the highlights — aside from seeing them all, of course! — is the hotel breakfasts. That's because there is nothing in the world like an Israeli hotel breakfast. Forget your bacon and sausages — meat is never present. Instead, there are endless dishes of different delicious salads, pickles of every hue, white cheeses topped with different herbs and spices, huge bowls of olives, eggs, different kinds of cured fish, pastries. . . It is simply fantastic. These slow-roasted tomatoes appeared on the buffet the last time I was there and I loved them: they are great for breakfast but equally good with any grilled or roasted meat or fish, or tossed with pasta or couscous, or on top of toasted sourdough with labneh (see page 142) or hummus. They will, I am sure, become as much part of your repertoire as they are mine.

**Serves 6**

12 tomatoes, halved
4 garlic cloves, cut into thin slivers
1 tbsp olive oil
salt and freshly ground black pepper
2 tbsp za'atar

Preheat the oven to 120°C/Gas ½ and line a baking sheet with baking parchment.

Toss the tomato halves and garlic in the olive oil and season with salt and pepper. Arrange them on the lined baking sheet, cut-side up. Sprinkle over the za'atar.

Roast for 2½ hours, or until they are shrivelled and very soft. Serve at room temperature.

# Roasted aubergine with pomegranate & tahini yoghurt dressing

I have no hesitation in naming aubergine as my favourite vegetable, particularly when it is roasted, and this is one of my favourite ways to serve it. The two dressings are great together here, but feel free to drop the yoghurt if you want a dairy-free version.

**Serves 4–6**

2 aubergines (about 500g in total), cut into 1cm rounds
about 100ml olive oil
salt and freshly ground black pepper
100g walnuts, broken into small pieces
2 tbsp pomegranate molasses
2 tbsp tahini
4 tbsp Greek-style yoghurt
2 tbsp lemon juice
150g rocket leaves
100g pomegranate seeds
a small handful of mint leaves, chopped

Preheat the oven to 200°C/Gas 6 and line a baking sheet with baking parchment.

Take the aubergine slices and brush them generously on each side with olive oil. Lay them on the lined baking sheet, season well with salt and pepper, and roast for about 45 minutes, until golden brown.

Put the walnuts on a separate small baking sheet and place in the oven for the last 10 minutes of cooking time. Remove both the aubergine slices and walnuts from the oven and allow to cool to room temperature.

Mix the pomegranate molasses with the tahini and loosen with about 4 tablespoons of water; season to taste. In a separate bowl mix the yoghurt with the lemon juice and a pinch of salt.

To assemble the dish, arrange the rocket leaves on a serving plate and top with the aubergine slices. Place blobs of the yoghurt dressing over the salad and drizzle over the tahini dressing. Sprinkle with the toasted walnuts and pomegranate seeds, top with chopped mint leaves and serve immediately.

# Spelt with butternut squash, cranberries & basil

I am not someone who buys many ready-made products but I do love a shortcut and I'm a HUGE fan of ready-cooked grains, including spelt and quinoa. I have lost count of the numbers of times I have wanted supper in a hurry and simply opened one of those packets, added some leftover chicken or salmon, a chopped avocado, a load of cherry tomatoes and a bag of rocket or spinach, squeezed over a lemon and had a great meal ready in minutes. You can cook the spelt from scratch and let it cool if you want to, but why bother? Oh, and I cheat with the squash, too!

**Serves 6**

125g spelt (or use a 250g pouch of cooked spelt)
1 butternut squash, peeled and cut into chunks (or 400g prepared squash)
1 garlic clove, unpeeled
2 red onions, cut into wedges
2 tbsp olive oil
salt and freshly ground black pepper
a pinch of chilli flakes
100g dried cranberries
100g pistachios, shelled
a small bunch of basil leaves, picked off the stems but kept whole
a small bunch of flat-leaf parsley, roughly chopped
85g baby spinach leaves
150g mild goats' cheese, crumbled (*optional*)

FOR THE DRESSING
4 tbsp balsamic vinegar
4 tbsp extra-virgin olive oil
1 tbsp wholegrain mustard
1 tbsp date syrup (*silan*) or honey
salt and freshly ground black pepper

Preheat the oven to 200°C/Gas 6.

If you are cooking the spelt from scratch, rinse the grains thoroughly in cold water and add to a pan with enough cold water to cover the grains. Bring to the boil then reduce the heat and simmer for 20 minutes, or until tender. Drain, rinse in cold water and drain again.

Put the butternut squash in a bowl with the garlic clove and red onion wedges, pour over the olive oil, season well and toss to coat. Tip into a roasting tray, sprinkle over the chilli flakes and roast for 40 minutes, or until the squash and onions are tender and browning at the edges. Remove from the oven and allow to cool slightly, then remove the garlic clove and set aside for the dressing.

Put the spelt into a large bowl with all the other ingredients. Mix well. Add the roasted vegetables and toss again.

Stir together the dressing ingredients in a bowl and squeeze in the roasted garlic clove, discarding the skin. Season and mix well, making sure the garlic has been broken up and dispersed through the dressing.

Pour the dressing over the salad, toss well, and serve immediately. Alternatively, you can keep the salad covered in the fridge, without pouring over the dressing, for up to 24 hours. Bring to room temperature, adding the dressing before serving.

# Israeli salad

Israeli salad is served everywhere and with everything in Israel: alongside a breakfast omelette; inside a huge Iraqi-style flatbread with lamb shawarma; or as a main course topped with garlicky chicken or scattered with crumbled white cheese. It is essentially chopped tomatoes and cucumbers, dressed with lemon juice, but as you might expect, there are dozens of variations. Here is my favourite.

**Serves 6**

2 cucumbers
6 firm, ripe tomatoes, diced
1 red onion, finely chopped
1 red pepper, deseeded and diced
1 yellow pepper, deseeded and diced
a small handful of mint leaves, chopped
a large handful of flat-leaf parsley leaves, chopped
a small handful of pomegranate seeds
juice of 1 lemon
2 tbsp extra-virgin olive oil
a pinch of ground cinnamon
a good pinch of salt

Halve the cucumbers lengthways and use a teaspoon to remove the seeds and watery centre. Then cut the cucumbers into thin strips and then into dice.

Put all the ingredients in a bowl, in the order listed, leaving the lemon juice, olive oil, cinnamon and salt until just before serving. Toss together, then taste and season with a little more salt if necessary. Serve immediately, at room temperature.

# Latkes

Latkes are like the best-ever crispy hash brown combined with a deep, fluffy potato pancake. Perhaps the reason they taste so darned good is because I only eat them once a year, at Chanukah, when it is traditional for Jewish people to eat deep-fried foods because of a miracle involving oil (it's a long but pretty exciting story. Look it up under 'Maccabees'). Yup, we have a festival that involves eating doughnuts. It was only when I was on holiday in America over Chanukah a few years ago that I discovered that there they are served with cinnamon, apple sauce and sour cream. Here, they are way more savoury, served on the side of a salt beef sandwich or with hot dogs. They're also great as a starter topped with smoked salmon and crème fraîche, like a blini, or with fried eggs on top. Also, you could swap some of the potato for sweet potato and beetroot. Whatever way you serve them, you need some latkes in your life.

**Makes 12–16
depending on size**

600g potatoes, peeled
1 large onion
1 tbsp plain flour
2 tbsp medium matzah meal or dried
  breadcrumbs
1 egg, beaten
1½ tsp salt
½ tsp ground white pepper (use black if
  you don't have white)
sunflower oil (or other flavourless oil),
  for frying

Coarsely grate the potatoes using the large holes of a box grater. Then grate the onion using the small holes of the grater, so they are almost like a paste. (Alternatively, to cut down on tears, use a food processor for the grating!) Tip onto a clean tea towel and pull up the edges so the potatoes and onion are in a ball at the bottom then squeeze as hard as you can over the sink to remove as much liquid as possible.

Tip the potatoes and onion into a bowl and add the flour, matzah meal or breadcrumbs, egg, salt and pepper and stir well to combine.

Pour the oil into a high-sided frying pan to a depth of 3cm. Heat until a cube of bread dropped into the oil sizzles and turns golden in 30 seconds. Line a rack or plate with kitchen paper.

Working in batches, drop tablespoons of the mixture into the oil and fry until browned, then turn them over to make sure the other side is browned, too – it will take about 5 minutes in total. Drain on the lined rack or plate and sprinkle with salt while you continue cooking the rest. Serve hot.

# Slow-cooked garlicky green beans

I love a vegetable accompaniment that I can make in advance and then just heat up to serve rather than faffing with pans while everyone is sitting at the table. These braised, garlicky beans in a rich tomato sauce – versions of which are popular all over the Mediterranean and Middle East – are something I serve regularly with a roast chicken. The dish is great for a crowd, and is actually better if made the day or morning before and then reheated.

**Serves 4**

2 tbsp olive oil
1 large onion, finely chopped
3 garlic cloves, very thinly sliced
450g green beans, topped and tailed
1 x 400g tin of chopped tomatoes
1 tbsp tomato purée
1 tbsp lemon juice
75ml water
¼ tsp ground allspice
½ tsp caster sugar
salt and freshly ground black pepper

Heat the oil in a pan over a low heat. Add the onion and cook gently for 10–15 minutes, or until translucent and soft, stirring occasionally. Add the garlic and cook very gently for a further 5 minutes, so it softens but does not colour.

Add the green beans, chopped tomatoes, tomato purée and lemon juice, along with the water to loosen. Stir well to combine. Add the allspice and caster sugar and season with salt and pepper. Bring to the boil then simmer for 40 minutes, until the beans are tender.

Cool and chill until ready to use, then reheat. Check the seasoning before serving warm.

# Dips,
# Pickles &
# Nibbles

# My favourite pita toppings

As well as being the perfect pocket, suitable for stuffing with lamb, chicken, falafel and endless salads, I often use pieces of pita as scoops for dips, like hummus and matbucha (see pages 184 and 180). However, it has another use that I feel is overlooked: it works as a delicious base for toppings — anything from fried lamb mince to melted cheese works a treat.

I find that the best route to success with this is to brush one side of the bread with olive oil, add your toppings and then warm through in the oven at 180°C/Gas 4 for 3–4 minutes. You will instantly transform a mezze platter or a bowl of soup — or they can be a supper in their own right, a bit like a mini pizza. Here are a few ideas for how to pimp your pita!

- **Za'atar**

The most straightforward topping is za'atar (hyssop or wild thyme), which you can buy in the spice sections of many supermarkets as well as Middle Eastern grocery shops, where it is usually blended with sesame seeds and sumac — a bright pink, wild berry with a citrus flavour that is dried and crushed.

Brush the pita with olive oil, dust evenly with za'atar and warm through in the oven — or warm the pita first, spread with labneh (Middle Eastern strained yoghurt — see page 142 for a recipe) or Greek yoghurt, and sprinkle the za'atar on top.

- **Sesame seeds**

These are used liberally on bread in the Middle East — far more so than the meagre sprinklings you see on loaves here. Tip sesame seeds on to a plate then press your olive oil-brushed pita on to the plate so the seeds stick all over it. Bake for a few minutes and serve.

- **Rosemary & rock salt**

This only works if you can find some fairly soft rosemary — not the horrid, dry spiky stuff. Pull the leaves away from the tough stems and sprinkle a few over the oiled pita — not too many or it will start to taste bitter — and sprinkle with a pinch of sea salt flakes. Warm through and munch. Beats crisps!

- **Feta & sumac**

Brush your pita with olive oil then bake until warm. Crumble feta finely all over the warm pita — like a thin layer of snow. Sprinkle the sumac in a bright pink, diagonal stripe across the middle for maximum dramatic effect.

- **Sundried tomato paste, black olives & basil**

So. . . this is basically the pizza pimp. As well as sundried tomato paste, olives and basil, which I see as pretty essential, add any other bits you would usually have on a pizza. For me, that involves piling on capers and anchovies with abandon, while my daughters like mozzarella and mushrooms. Drizzle a little olive oil on top after the toppings, then warm through.

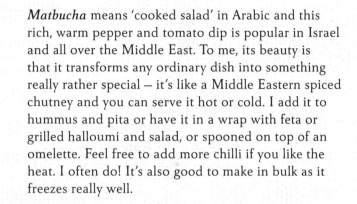

# Matbucha
## (spiced pepper & tomato dip)

*Matbucha* means 'cooked salad' in Arabic and this rich, warm pepper and tomato dip is popular in Israel and all over the Middle East. To me, its beauty is that it transforms any ordinary dish into something really rather special – it's like a Middle Eastern spiced chutney and you can serve it hot or cold. I add it to hummus and pita or have it in a wrap with feta or grilled halloumi and salad, or spooned on top of an omelette. Feel free to add more chilli if you like the heat. I often do! It's also good to make in bulk as it freezes really well.

**Serves 8**

2 red peppers
2 green chillies (fat ones, like jalapeños)
5 ripe tomatoes (or use 1 x 400g tin of chopped tomatoes)
4 garlic cloves, crushed
1 tbsp olive oil
1 tsp hot paprika
a pinch of chilli flakes (*optional*)
½ tsp sugar
½ tsp salt
1 tbsp tomato purée
salt and freshly ground black pepper

First, roast the peppers and chillies, either under the grill or by holding them with tongs over the open flame on your hob, until the skin is totally charred black all over. Place them in a glass bowl, cover with cling film and leave to cool, then rub off the skins and roughly chop the peppers and chillies, discarding the membranes and seeds.

While the peppers and chillies are charring, you can prepare your tomatoes (if using fresh ones). Cut a cross in the bottom of each one with a sharp knife, then place them in a pan of boiling water. After 10 seconds, scoop them into a bowl of iced water or run them under the tap in a sieve. You can now remove the skins, which should have become loose. Halve, discard the seeds, and dice the flesh.

OK. Faff over. Now you just put the peppers, chillies and tomatoes in a pan with all the remaining ingredients and let everything simmer gently over a low heat for about an hour, depending on how juicy your tomatoes are, stirring from time to time, or until most of the liquid has evaporated and you are left with a pan of thick, shiny, unctuous, red loveliness.

Taste and adjust the seasoning. Serve at room temperature as part of a mezze or with anything that needs a little livening up. Keep in the fridge for up to a week or in the freezer for up to 3 months.

# Chatzilim
## (aubergine salad)

So, once you get into charring aubergines, your life will never be the same again. You can do SO MUCH with them. Mix the lovely squishy middle with tahini, mayonnaise, cumin, garlic, chopped red onions, grated tomatoes, goats' cheese, chopped fresh herbs. . . Seriously, I could write a whole book of things to do with charred aubergines. Instead, I am giving you just one mezze dish. Do not feel deprived; you will love it.

**Serves 8**

2 aubergines
½ cucumber
1 red pepper, deseeded and finely chopped
1 yellow pepper, deseeded and finely chopped
2 tomatoes, finely chopped
1 small red onion, finely chopped
seeds of ½ pomegranate (or buy a pot of seeds and use about 3 tbsp), plus extra to garnish
1 tbsp olive oil
2 tbsp lemon juice
salt and freshly ground black pepper
a small handful of chopped flat-leaf parsley
a small handful of chopped dill fronds

Char the aubergines over the open flame of your hob. (TOP TIP! If you remove the rack from the hob and put foil underneath it you will have very little mess to clear up afterwards.) Use tongs to turn the aubergines gently so they are charred all over. When the aubergine skins are scorched and they have started to collapse, allow them to cool slightly, then cut them in half with a sharp knife and scoop out the meltingly soft centres. Chop the flesh and place it in a bowl, discarding the burnt skins.

While the aubergines are cooling, cut the cucumber in half lengthways and use a teaspoon to scoop out and discard the seeds. Finely chop and then add to the aubergine flesh along with the peppers, tomatoes, red onion and pomegranate seeds. Dress with the olive oil and lemon juice and season to taste with salt and black pepper. Mix well.

At this point, you can cover and refrigerate for 3–4 days. Just before serving, add the chopped herbs and garnish with a few more pomegranate seeds.

Chatzilim
page 181

Hummus
page 184

Matbucha
page 180

# Hummus

Hummus purists will only make it with dried chickpeas, soaked overnight, but I have no foresight so I always make mine with tinned (gasp!) and it's still a delight. To be honest, I think the key is in the tahini more than the chickpeas anyway. Never buy the grey sludge in jars; buy the tahini that comes in plastic containers with Arabic or Hebrew writing on the front from the international sections of supermarkets or Middle Eastern grocers. Dropping ice cubes into the food processor does something very clever to the hummus. I am not clear on exactly HOW it does this, but believe me, it gives it the consistency of freshly churned ice cream, as well as a beautiful pale hue. Always let your hummus come up to room temperature before serving.

**Serves 6**

1 x 400g tin of chickpeas, rinsed and
    drained
1 garlic clove, crushed
150g tahini, plus extra to serve
75ml very cold water
juice of ½ lemon
3 tbsp olive oil, plus extra to serve
½ tsp salt
4 ice cubes
sumac, to garnish (*optional*)

Tip the chickpeas into a food processor with the garlic and whizz until the chickpeas are completely broken down to a fine gravel-like consistency. Then add all the other ingredients, except the ice cubes, and whizz again for a minute or two.

Add the ice cubes one at a time down the chute of the food processor, with the motor still running. You will see the hummus become pale and creamy. Keep whizzing until you have a hummus that is the consistency you like – add a little more water if you like (not oil – it will just emulsify and make it thicker). Taste and adjust the seasoning with more salt or lemon juice.

To serve, spread the hummus over a small plate, make a crater in the middle, pour in a little extra tahini and drizzle with olive oil and garnish with sumac, if you like. If not using immediately, cover and refrigerate for up to a week.

 Variations:

- *Top with warm lamb mince, sautéed with salt, pepper and parsley and a teaspoon of harissa.*

- *Top with a couple of tablespoons of warm chickpeas and hot sauce.*

- *Top with a mixture of finely chopped onion, chopped pickled Middle Eastern chillies (or jalapeños) and chopped fresh parsley.*

# Egg & onion

How something so simple became such an emblematic dish of Jewish delis, I do not know. It also bewilders me how there can be so many variations of the same dish. You can use spring onions or brown onions, cooked or raw and bind the mixture with butter or chicken fat or mayonnaise. Here's how we always do it in my house.

**Serves 6**

6 hard-boiled eggs, peeled
6 spring onions, finely chopped, including
   the softer parts of the green stems
1 tbsp good-quality mayonnaise
salt and ground white pepper

Grate the eggs using the large holes of a box grater. Add to a bowl, mix with the spring onions and stir in the mayonnaise.

Season generously with salt and pepper (it needs to be highly seasoned because when it is served straight from the fridge it can be very bland). Cover and refrigerate for up to 2 days before using.

Serve with matzah crackers or challah and chopped liver (see page 186) – or in a bagel with smoked salmon.

# Chopped liver

My grandma used to make this coarse paté almost every week for our starter on Friday nights, frying the onions and livers in schmaltz (chicken fat), which filled her house with the most divine smell. I remember standing on a stool and turning the handle of the cast-iron mincer that lived on her kitchen work surface. These days I use a food processor and sunflower oil, which is speedier and healthier – though it will never taste as good as Grandma's.

**Serves 6**

2 tbsp sunflower oil
2 large onions, chopped
225g chicken livers (or use a mixture
    of chicken and calves' liver)
4 hard-boiled eggs, peeled
salt and ground white pepper

Heat the oil in a frying pan. Add the onions and fry over a medium heat until they are golden, about 10 minutes.

Trim the chicken livers to remove any sinew. Chop roughly then add to the onions and fry slowly for 5 minutes, until they have turned brown and started to fall apart in the pan. This is not a moment for under-cooked, fashionably pink-centred livers, but you don't want them hard and chewy either, so cook them gently.

Let the onions and livers cool, then use a slotted spoon to transfer them to a food processor, keeping most of the oil in the pan. Add the eggs to the food processor. Pulse gently until you have a coarse paté. (You can also do this by chopping everything on a board with a large knife and mixing it all together in a bowl.)

Stir in a little of the oil used for cooking, taste and season well with salt and pepper. Keep, covered, in the fridge for up to 2 days.

Serve with matzah crackers (or water biscuits) and egg and onion (see page 185). It's also absolutely fantastic in a challah sandwich with leftover cold roast chicken, sliced pickled cucumbers and English mustard.

# Chopped herring

Chopped herring sounds pretty dreadful, doesn't it? How about chopped herring with apples, onion and hard-boiled eggs? Don't turn the page just yet – believe me, chopped herring is one of the delights of the Jewish kitchen. In fact, chopped herring on toasted rye bread, as well as being utterly heavenly, is one of the best hangover cures I know. Maybe the Russians or Poles of yesteryear invented it after a night on the vodka. . .

## Serves 6

1 jar (about 300g) of pickled herrings (sometimes labelled marinated herrings) or rollmops
1 small mild onion
1 small apple (something tart like a Cox is good)
3 hard-boiled eggs, peeled
3 tbsp fresh breadcrumbs
a few dill fronds
2 tbsp lemon juice
1 tsp caster sugar, or to taste
salt and freshly ground black pepper

Drain the herrings well, using kitchen paper to get them as dry as possible.

You can chop everything by hand but it is much easier with a food processor, which is what I recommend you use.

Pulse the onion in a food processor until it is finely chopped but not yet a paste. Core and roughly chop the apple (keep the peel on) and add that, along with the herring; pulse until finely chopped, too. Now add the eggs, breadcrumbs and dill fronds, along with the lemon juice and sugar and pulse again.

Taste and season with salt and pepper and a little more caster sugar, if needed. Transfer to a bowl, cover and refrigerate for up to 3 days. Serve with rye bread or bagels – it's also delicious on toasted granary bread.

# New green pickled cucumbers

I have very strong memories of when I was little, going to see my much-loved granddad at his chicken shop on Jubilee Street, in the East End of London, and going into a grocery shop nearby where we fished pickles out of barrels and took them home in plastic bags. These days, good old 'elf and safety has put an end to pickles in barrels in shops and I have never got round to making them at home because I didn't really like the idea of having them frothing as they fermented in the garage. But I do love pickles and enjoy making the non-fermented type. These fresh pickles, known as 'new greens' because they are made with young cucumbers and keep their green colour, are super quick, very easy and totally delicious. If you can, do use small, firm cucumbers, which are better at keeping their crunch than standard salad cucumbers. You can find them in some supermarkets and greengrocers and in Middle Eastern shops.

## Makes 4 x 500ml jars

800g small, firm cucumbers
  (or use bigger ones)
250ml distilled malt vinegar
1 litre water
2 tbsp salt
2 tbsp caster sugar
4 garlic cloves, peeled
a small bunch of dill
4 bay leaves
1 tbsp black peppercorns
1 tsp coriander seeds
½ tsp caraway seeds
½ tsp chilli flakes

If you can find small, firm cucumbers, cut them into large chunks. If not, halve the cucumbers lengthways and use a teaspoon to scoop out the seeds, then cut into chunky slices, about 3cm thick.

Put the vinegar, water, salt, sugar and garlic in a large pan and bring to the boil; boil for 1 minute. This should stop the garlic turning blue in the jars and will also make sure the sugar and salt are dissolved and help the pickling process begin.

Make sure your jars are clean — I run mine through the dishwasher before using, which sterilises them. Into each jar place a quarter of the dill, 1 bay leaf, 1 boiled garlic clove and a quarter of the other spices (it's easier if you mix them together first and then divide the mixture between the jars).

Now add the cucumbers, cramming as many into each jar as possible. Fill up the jars with the hot pickling liquid (this is easier if you transfer it to a jug first). Screw the lids on the jars, allow to cool slightly, and put in the fridge.

You can eat these after 24 hours but they'll be better after 48. They will keep for a week once opened and for about 3 weeks if left unopened.

# Quick pickled red onions

These are fantastic fun — they take no time to make and you can eat them almost immediately, although I recommend you leave them for 2 hours at least. An unopened jar will last for about 6 months in the fridge but they are best eaten the week they are made. I love to serve them with smoked mackerel paté and toast as a starter, but they are great with cold roast chicken or even in a cheese sandwich. You can totally mix up the spices — juniper berries or coriander seeds work really well in place of the allspice, and the addition of cloves or cinnamon is good, too.

**Makes 1 x 500g jar**

2 red onions, sliced into rings
360ml white wine vinegar
100g golden caster sugar
2 tsp salt
6 black peppercorns
5 allspice berries
1 star anise
1 bay leaf
1 small dried red chilli (*optional*)

Boil the kettle and put the onion slices in a sieve. Pour boiling water over the onion slices and drain well. Allow to cool while you make the spiced vinegar.

Pour the vinegar into a small pan and add the sugar, salt, peppercorns, allspice, star anise, bay leaf and chilli, if using. Place over a medium heat and bring to a simmer for a minute, just until the sugar and salt have dissolved.

Pack the onion rings into a 500g sterilised jar (putting the jar through the dishwasher does the trick) and pour over the hot, spiced vinegar.

Put the lid on and allow to cool before refrigerating. Leave for at least 30 minutes, ideally 2 hours and for up to 6 months. Once opened, keep in the fridge and eat within 2 weeks.

# Chraine

Chraine is a relish made from beetroot, horseradish, vinegar and sugar. It's definitely NOT one of those things you want to eat by the spoonful from the jar, but it is fantastic with gefilte fish (see page 36), or you can mix it with mayo to create 'chrayonnaise', which livens up a piece of poached salmon or a turkey sandwich no end! Most people buy it — it's readily available in supermarkets now — but it is easy to make, particularly as fresh horseradish seems to be increasingly available. Beware though, horseradish is incredibly pungent until mixed with the vinegar. It's easiest to make this in a food processor where the lid will help protect your eyes; just look away when you first open it. It will also help protect your hands from the pink stains of the beetroot; wear gloves when you peel them.

### Makes about 3 x 450g jars

4 beetroot, scrubbed
10cm piece of fresh horseradish,
    peeled and cut into rough chunks
2 tbsp granulated sugar
50ml white wine vinegar
1 tbsp lemon juice
1 tsp salt
100ml water

Place the beetroot in a small pan, cover with water and bring to the boil. Reduce the heat and simmer until they are tender, about 30 minutes. Drain and leave to cool.

When the beetroot are cool enough to handle, peel off the skins, which should slip away if you rub them. Remember to wear gloves! Cut into rough chunks and put into a food processor with the horseradish.

In the meantime, put the sugar in a small pan with the vinegar, lemon juice, salt and the water. Bring slowly to the boil to dissolve the sugar, then remove from the heat.

Turn the food processor on so it starts chopping the beetroot and horseradish. Through the funnel of the processor, drizzle the vinegar-sugar-lemon-juice mixture. When the liquid is all in and the beetroot and horseradish have a paste-like consistency, stop the motor.

Spoon the chraine into sterilised jars (I run them through the dishwasher, which does the trick). Refrigerate for at least 24 hours and keep in the fridge for up to 3 weeks. Once opened, use within 2 weeks.

# Bread & butter pickles

I get a bit emotional talking about these pickles. I very nearly started a pickle company with a fantastic, equally pickle-crazy friend, Andrew Sinclair, who now lives in New York. The company didn't happen — or hasn't yet — but one of the first products we developed was this one for cucumber slices in a sweet brine that is almost like a syrup. Apparently these are called bread and butter pickles because during the Great Depression in America, home-grown cucumbers, pickled like this and eaten with bread and butter was all many people could afford to eat. Don't let that fool you — they are delicious and perfect with cheese, meats or anything, really.

**Makes 2 x 500ml jars**

800g cucumbers (ideally small and thick-
    skinned; look for them in Middle Eastern
    shops or large supermarkets), thinly sliced
2 red onions, thinly sliced
4 tbsp rock salt
600ml cider vinegar
280g caster sugar
1 tsp ground turmeric
1 tbsp yellow mustard seeds
1 tsp coriander seeds
1 tsp celery seeds
1 mild red chilli, very thinly sliced

Put the cucumber and onion slices in a bowl and toss with the salt. Cover with a clean tea towel and leave for 3 hours at room temperature, then rinse well in cold water and drain. Dry in the tea towel, squeezing gently to remove any excess liquid.

Put all the other ingredients in a pan and slowly bring to the boil. Add the cucumber and onion slices, stir well and bring back to the boil, then let everything bubble together for a few minutes.

Remove from the heat and then carefully fill the sterilised jars (putting them through the dishwasher does the trick). Put the lids on and cool. Refrigerate until ready to use. They will keep in the fridge, unopened, for up to 3 weeks. Once opened, use within 2 weeks.

# Uncle Ike's piccalilli

My great-uncle Ike was a man of few words but was a fantastic artist; he and my great-auntie Naomi had a wonderful loft full of exciting things that they used to let me explore when I was a child. Among the astonishing array of buttons and boxes of artists' charcoal and stamps were always jars of piccalilli – or mustard pickle, as we called it – which was the only thing he cooked. We ate it with cold roast chicken, salt beef or slices of boiled tongue. This is his recipe, which he scribbled down on a piece of brown paper for my mum, before he died. I like to add a dried red chilli to the mixture – though it is a good idea to fish it out before you jar it.

**Makes 6 x 500g jars**

500g green beans, trimmed and cut in half
500g small pickling onions, skinned
500g marrow, cut into bite-sized chunks
500g cucumber, cut into bite-sized pieces
750g cauliflower, broken into small florets
100g salt
around 3 litres water
1.7 litres distilled malt vinegar
2 tbsp dried mustard powder
2 tsp ground ginger
1 dried chilli (*optional*)
250g granulated sugar
40g plain flour
4 tsp ground turmeric

Put the vegetables in a large, non-reactive bowl. Dissolve the salt in the water and pour it over the vegetables. There should be enough liquid to cover them – if not, add more water.

Put the vinegar into a large pan with the mustard powder, ginger and chilli, if using. Leave both the vegetables and the vinegar overnight at room temperature.

The next day, drain and rinse the vegetables thoroughly and then drain them again well. Add the sugar to the vinegar in the pan and bring to the boil. Add the vegetables and simmer for 20 minutes.

Remove the chilli if you have used one, then lift the vegetables out of the pan with a slotted spoon and pack into warm, sterilised jars (I run them through the dishwasher).

Mix the flour and turmeric to a smooth paste with a little of the vinegar. Stir this into the rest of the hot syrup. Boil for a few minutes until the paste is thick enough to coat the back of a spoon, then pour over the vegetables in the jars and seal the jars with vinegar-proof lids.

This is best left for 6 weeks before eating but it is – believe me – still delicious even after a fortnight. Once opened, it will keep for 2 weeks.

# Desserts

# Cheese blintzes with berry compote

Life should involve more blintzes. They are super-thin crêpes and can be sweet or savoury. My brother Howard, a food photographer and excellent cook, makes a brilliant version filled with minced roasted chicken. This sweet version, filled with a mixture of ricotta and cream cheese and served with a berry compote and sour cream, is a joy. You can make them the day before and fry the blintzes just before serving.

## Serves 4

FOR THE PANCAKES
100g plain flour
¼ tsp salt
1 tbsp caster sugar
2 eggs
100ml milk
100ml water
sunflower oil (or other flavourless oil),
    for frying
butter, for frying

FOR THE FILLING
250g ricotta
50g full-fat cream cheese
1 egg yolk
2 tbsp caster sugar
1 tsp vanilla extract
grated zest of 1 lemon
a pinch of salt

FOR THE COMPOTE
400g frozen mixed berries
60g caster sugar
juice of 1 lemon

sour cream, to serve (*optional*)

First, make the pancakes. If you have a food processor or blender, simply pop in all the ingredients and whizz to a smooth batter. If not, put the flour, salt and sugar in a bowl, mix together and make a well in the centre. Mix together the eggs, milk, water and 2 teaspoons of oil in a jug and pour slowly into the well. Use a wooden spoon to stir, gradually bringing in the flour from the sides, to create a smooth batter. Pour the batter into a jug and set aside for 30 minutes (or put in the fridge overnight if it's more convenient).

To make the filling, blend all the ingredients in a food processor or blender (or use a handheld electric whisk), and set aside.

For the compote, put the ingredients into a small pan set over a medium heat for about 5 minutes, until the berries start to collapse.

To cook the pancakes, put a teaspoon of oil in a 15cm non-stick pan (you can use another size but this is the perfect size for blintzes) over a medium heat. Wipe the oil over the base of the pan with kitchen paper then add a knob of butter. When it is foaming, use a ladle to pour just enough batter into the pan to coat the base. You can make the layer quite thick but as soon as it starts to set, pour any excess batter that has not set back into the bowl. This way you will get super-thin pancakes. As soon as it starts to curl up from the sides of the pan and turn brown, turn it on to a plate and cover with a piece of greaseproof paper. You are only cooking one side of the crêpe at this stage. Continue until you have about eight pancakes.

Now fill the pancakes. Put a pancake, cooked-side up, on a board. Spread a tablespoon of filling along the bottom half. Fold the bottom of the pancake up, fold in the sides, and fold over into a parcel. Repeat with all the pancakes and filling. (The filled blintzes can be chilled in the fridge overnight at this point.)

Heat a good knob of butter and 2 teaspoons of sunflower oil in a large frying pan. Put in the blintzes and fry on both sides until golden brown. You can keep them warm in a low oven for up to 15 minutes if that's helpful. Serve with compote and sour cream.

# Knafeh
## (Israeli cheesecake with shredded filo)

If you walk through Carmel Market in Tel Aviv you will see stalls selling giant pans full of *knafeh* – an Arabic dessert that has a creamy middle and a crunchy top and bottom from the shredded filo that gives it its name. It is soaked in syrup flavoured either with rose water or orange blossom and often the pastry is dyed a garish orange – though I don't do that. You can find *knafeh* dough in the freezers of Middle Eastern grocery shops and it is really easy to use. If you can't get hold of it you can use crushed cornflakes – it sounds strange but trust me! Traditionally the dessert is made from an unsalted cheese called *akkawi*, but a combination of ricotta and mozzarella works well, too.

**Serves 10**

450g *knafeh* dough (or use 300g
   crushed cornflakes)
200g butter, melted
400g mozzarella, coarsely grated
400g ricotta
1 tsp rose water
100g pistachios, crushed

FOR THE SYRUP
450g caster sugar
½ tsp lemon juice
½ tsp rose water
250ml water

Preheat the oven to 180°C/Gas 4.

Break the *knafeh* dough up by whizzing it in a food processor until the strands are no longer than grains of rice; you could also put it in a bag and bash it with a rolling pin. Tip into a bowl and then pour over the melted butter and make sure every strand is coated. Use your hands to really massage it in.

Press half the butter-coated pastry in the bottom of a 23cm ovenproof dish. Use your palms and fists to really push it down so it reaches the edges.

Mix the mozzarella with the ricotta and rose water in a bowl and spread this over the buttery *knafeh* in an even layer. Spread the remaining *knafeh* over the cheese mixture and press it down gently. Bake for about 1 hour, or until golden brown and crunchy on top.

Meanwhile, make the syrup. Combine the sugar, lemon juice, rose water and the water in a small pan and heat gently until the sugar has dissolved. Simmer over a low heat for about 10 minutes, or until you have a glossy syrup that coats the back of a spoon. Remove from the heat, cool and then chill in the fridge.

When the *knafeh* comes out of the oven, immediately pour over the cold syrup and sprinkle the pistachios over the top. Traditionally *knafeh* is served warm, straight from the oven, but I love it cold, too, served with mint tea, like baklava.

# Halva, pistachio & dark chocolate ice cream

This easy, no-churn ice cream method needs a drum roll if you haven't come across it before. It's been picked up by a number of chefs and it's so clever it almost shouldn't be allowed. You just mix condensed milk with double cream, pop it in the freezer and you're done! You can add whatever you like to the basic recipe but the ingredients I've used here elevate it to another level. Halva is a crumbly, sesame-based confectionery, popular across the Middle East – and now that you can find it in supermarkets, there's no excuse not to use it at every opportunity.

**Serves 8**

600ml double cream
200ml sweetened condensed milk
1 tsp vanilla extract
250g halva, crumbled
100g dark chocolate, coarsely grated
100g pistachios, finely chopped or
    coarsely ground in a food processor

TO DECORATE (OPTIONAL)
50g dark chocolate, melted
a small handful of crushed pistachios
1 tbsp sesame seeds

Put the double cream, condensed milk and vanilla extract in a large bowl and use a handheld electric whisk to whisk until thick and stiffened. This should take about 3–4 minutes.

Fold in the halva, grated chocolate and chopped pistachios.

Pour the mixture into a plastic container or large loaf tin and cover with cling film. Freeze until solid, about 5 hours (or you can freeze it overnight).

Remove from the freezer about 20 minutes before you want to serve it. Decorate by drizzling some melted dark chocolate over the top and sprinkling with crushed pistachios and sesame seeds, if liked.

# Apple &
# fig bread
# & butter
# pudding

I have two lovely old, gnarled apple trees in my garden that heave with fruit in the autumn despite my ignoring them the rest of the year, so I am forever looking for new ways to use apples in desserts. After a traditional Jewish Friday night dinner, we often have this delicious take on a classic bread and butter pudding because it uses ceremonial sweet wine to plump up the dried fruit (although sherry or orange juice work just as well) and brioche-like challah. You can also make it dairy-free, which observant Jews require after a meat main course.

**Serves 6–8**

75g dried figs, chopped
50g raisins
50g dried cranberries
75ml Kiddush wine, sweet sherry
   or orange juice
300g challah or other white bread, sliced
100g butter (or use dairy-free spread)
2 apples, peeled, cored, chopped into small
   cubes and tossed in 1 tbsp lemon juice
75g granulated sugar
50g soft light brown sugar
½ tsp ground cinnamon
a pinch of ground cloves
350ml milk (or use dairy-free milk)
100ml double cream (or use dairy-free
   cream), plus extra to serve
3 eggs, beaten
1 tsp vanilla extract
grated zest of 1 lemon

Put the dried figs, raisins and cranberries in a small bowl and pour over the wine, sherry or orange juice. Let stand for half an hour, while you prepare everything else.

Spread the bread on both sides with butter or dairy-free spread, then cut into cubes (this is easiest if you stack the slices of buttered bread one on top of the other as you go, then slice in three one way and in three the other way to end up with nine cubes per slice). Tip the bread into a bowl, add the apples and mix to combine. Mix both sugars with the cinnamon and cloves, sprinkle over the bread and mix again. Tip into an ovenproof dish.

Mix the dried fruit, along with the soaking liquid, with the milk, cream, beaten eggs, vanilla extract and lemon zest. Pour over the bread and leave to soak for 30 minutes or up to a few hours.

When you are ready to cook the pudding, preheat the oven to 180°C/Gas 4. Bake for around 40 minutes, or until the custard has set and the top is a lovely golden brown. Serve warm with more cream or cold the next day for breakfast. (Or is that just me. . . ?)

# Plum & vanilla crumble

Like many other Jewish cooks, I tend to make a full three-course meal every Friday night to mark the Sabbath, particularly if I have friends or extended family over for dinner. A dessert that can be made in an instant after work, that never fails and is a real crowd-pleaser, is therefore a crucial part of my repertoire. This is a fantastic crumble, perfect for any time of year – though particularly in early autumn when British plums are at their best – and is just as good with apples, pears, rhubarb, peaches or a mixture of different fruit, depending on what I happen to have in the fruit bowl or fridge that week.

**Serves 8**

12 plums, stoned and quartered
1 tsp vanilla extract
4 tbsp maple syrup
1 tsp mixed spice
grated zest of 1 orange
2 tbsp water
1 tbsp ground almonds
custard or ice cream, to serve

FOR THE CRUMBLE TOPPING
250g plain flour
50g porridge oats
150g butter or margarine
150g soft light brown sugar

Preheat the oven to 200°C/Gas 6.

Put the plums in a bowl with the vanilla extract, maple syrup, mixed spice, orange zest, water and the ground almonds. Mix well to combine. Tip into a suitable ovenproof dish (you want it about half-full with the plum mixture) and roast the plums for 10 minutes.

Meanwhile, put the flour, oats, butter or margarine and brown sugar in a food processor and pulse until the ingredients start clumping together and you have a crumble mixture.

Sprinkle the crumble mixture over the cooked plums and cook for a further 30 minutes, until golden brown and bubbling at the edges. Remove from the oven and leave for 10 minutes before serving with custard or ice cream.

# Oranges with pomegranates, mint & ginger syrup

This is an updated version of the classic oranges in caramel my mum always made when she had a dinner party when I was young. The next morning, she would let me have a couple of leftover slices with my breakfast, which felt so special. It looks absolutely stunning; the vibrant orange slivers dotted with specks of ruby pomegranate and emerald mint leaves, like a wonderful bejewelled platter.

**Serves 6**

8 oranges
2 tbsp syrup from a jar of stem ginger
100g pomegranate seeds
a small handful of mint leaves, shredded

Peel the oranges, removing as much pith as possible or, if you have a bit more time and want to do something special for your guests, you can carefully pare them: with a serrated fruit knife, cut the top and bottom off each orange so you can stand them up. Place an orange on a board and, with the knife, cut vertically to slice away the peel and pith, following the contours of the fruit to keep it as spherical as possible. Do this for each orange.

Cut the peeled oranges into thin slices, about 5mm thick. Remove any seeds.

Arrange the slices on a platter, drizzle with the ginger syrup and garnish with pomegranate seeds and shredded mint leaves.

Keep covered in the fridge until ready to serve.

# Sarah's whisky squares

My adorable, multi-talented sister-in-law, Sarah Raanan, who lives in Israel, gave me this recipe. It is fantastic — a fridge cake with a bit of a kick that is perfect to serve with coffee after a heavy dinner, when you want a morsel of something sweet rather than a huge pudding. It is also so easy that I happily let my daughters make it for me — always a bonus!

**Makes 16**

130g butter or margarine
4 tbsp golden syrup
4 tbsp cocoa powder
50ml whisky (or use orange juice)
2 x 250g packets speculoos biscuits, such as Lotus (or use ginger snaps)
200g dark chocolate, roughly chopped

Place the butter or margarine, syrup, cocoa and whisky in a small pan and melt over a low heat, stirring to combine. Remove from the heat. While it is cooling slightly, line a 20cm square brownie tin with baking parchment.

Put the biscuits in a plastic food bag and bash them with a rolling pin into small pieces (not crumbs). Add them to the pan and stir until really well combined. Press into the tin in an even layer.

Place the chocolate in a heatproof bowl and set over a pan of gently simmering water, making sure the bottom of the bowl doesn't touch the water. Stir until melted, then spread the chocolate over the top. Put the tin in the fridge until hard, about 2 hours. Cut into small squares with a sharp knife.

# Dairy–free cheesecake

I have a serious love of cheesecake. There were two in my last book and this is the second in this book (see page 204). The reason I have included a dairy-free one is because Jewish people do not serve milk and meat together so we are always looking for a good dessert to have after a roast chicken. This cheesecake is really fun – it is so easy to make and nobody can ever believe it is dairy free. It's even better with some berry compote (see page 200) or just served with fresh berries.

**Serves 6**

50g margarine, melted, plus extra
    for greasing
100g digestive biscuits
50g demerara sugar
450g vegan cream cheese
2 eggs, beaten
100g caster sugar
1 tbsp plain flour
grated zest and juice of 1 lemon
1 tsp vanilla extract

Preheat the oven to 180°C/Gas 4 and grease and line the base of a 20cm round springform cake tin with baking parchment.

Put the biscuits in a plastic bag and bash them with a rolling pin to crumbs. Tip into a bowl, add the demerara sugar and stir well. Add the melted margarine and stir again.

Spoon the mixture into the prepared tin, pressing it down well. Bake in the oven for 10 minutes then remove from the oven and reduce the oven temperature to 170°C/Gas 3.

Meanwhile, mix the cream cheese with the eggs using a handheld electric whisk. Beat in the sugar, flour, lemon zest and juice and vanilla extract. Pour on top of the biscuit base, then return to the oven to bake for 45 minutes.

Cool then refrigerate until you are ready to serve. Remove from the tin, cut into slices and serve with fruit compote or fresh berries.

# Kadorei shokolad
## (Israeli chocolate biscuit balls)

This is the easiest dessert ever — a one-bowl wonder, made and loved by kids and adults alike, rather like the Israeli equivalent of chocolate cornflake cakes. You can customise them as you please, like you would a chocolate truffle. They are great rolled in desiccated coconut or colourful sprinkles, or you can add nuts or dried fruit — whatever you fancy. I have made mine chocolate orange flavoured, because that's my thing, and I've added booze because that's my other thing, but you can leave that out if you like.

**Makes about 20**

150g Petit Buerre biscuits (or use any other plain biscuit, such as Rich Tea)
80g butter (or use margarine for a dairy-free version)
100g dark orange-flavoured chocolate, roughly chopped
2 tbsp Grand Marnier or Cointreau
grated zest of 1 orange, plus 1 tbsp orange juice
55g caster sugar
chocolate sprinkles, to coat

Crush the biscuits in a plastic bag with a rolling pin or pulse to crumbs (you are not looking for a powder consistency) in a food processor. Tip into a bowl.

Put the butter and chocolate in a heatproof bowl set over a pan of gently simmering water, making sure the bottom of the bowl doesn't touch the water. Stir to melt, then add the alcohol, orange zest, orange juice and caster sugar and stir to combine.

Pour this mixture on to the crumbs and stir well to combine. The mixture should clump together — use another spoonful of orange juice if you need to.

Form the mixture into truffle-sized balls, then roll them in chocolate sprinkles. Refrigerate until ready to serve.

# Middle Eastern mess

Never has there been a better reason to not worry about whether your pavlova is cracking in the oven than Eton Mess. My take on the British classic contains figs, date syrup and bashed up baklava along with shop-bought meringues and raspberries. Of course, you can make your own meringues (or use a cracked pavlova), but we all need recipes we can make in a hurry. The baklava is optional but fun and provides a great texture. Also, you can buy it in supermarkets now, and it's not expensive, so why not? (See page 2 for photograph of finished dish.)

**Serves 6**

300g mascarpone
150g Greek yoghurt
75g icing sugar, sifted
1 tbsp rose water
3 meringue nests, roughly smashed
    into pieces
6 plump figs, quartered
450g raspberries
2 tbsp date syrup (*silan*)
around 8 pieces of baklava, smashed
    with a rolling pin (*optional*)
100g pomegranate seeds
a small bunch of mint leaves, shredded

Stir together the mascarpone, Greek yoghurt, icing sugar and rose water in a bowl, until well combined and creamy.

Fold in the smashed meringue nests, figs and raspberries. Drizzle over the date syrup and broken baklava pieces, if using, and fold again.

Cover and chill in the fridge until ready to serve. Serve chilled, sprinkled with the pomegranate seeds and mint leaves.

# Breads
# & Bakes

# PBJ breakfast muffins

Only parents of young children know the hellishness of term-time weekdays. As well as getting your kids out the door fully clothed with hair plaited and teeth brushed, there is always something missing or broken or unexpected – some unfinished school project that was supposed to be in yesterday; an empty 2-litre plastic bottle suddenly desperately needed for an art class; broken swimming goggles that need to be replaced NOW and 'why didn't you read that letter that had to be signed, Mummy?' These breakfast muffins (along with my brilliant and much-loved au pair, Nikola) are a lifesaver on those days. They can be eaten in the car when everything has gone wrong and they always make me feel just a tiny bit smug when I'd otherwise feel like an abject failure. I know it looks like a lot of ingredients, but you basically just shove them all in a bowl and stir them up. Couldn't be easier. If you have gluten issues, you can replace the flour with ground almonds or almond flour (which is available in supermarkets and health food stores and is just very finely ground almonds) and leave out the bicarb, but you will need to add 100ml of orange juice.

**Makes 12**

190g plain flour
80g porridge oats
2 tbsp pumpkin seeds
2 tsp baking powder
½ tsp bicarbonate of soda
1 tsp ground cinnamon
1 tsp ground ginger
100g soft light brown sugar
1 egg, beaten
1 tsp vanilla extract
75g sultanas
3 bananas, mashed
2 tbsp peanut butter
2 tbsp sunflower oil
100g strawberry or raspberry jam

Preheat the oven to 180°C/Gas 4 and line a 12-hole muffin tin with paper cases.

In a large bowl, mix the flour with the oats, pumpkin seeds, baking powder, bicarbonate of soda, cinnamon, ginger and sugar until evenly combined. Add the beaten egg, vanilla, sultanas, mashed bananas, peanut butter and sunflower oil. Stir gently to combine but do not over mix or the muffins will be tough. Don't worry if the mixture is lumpy, just make sure there are no dry patches.

Half-fill each paper case with the mixture, then add a good teaspoon of strawberry or raspberry jam to each one. Spoon the rest of the muffin mixture over the top of the jam and then bake in the oven for 30 minutes, until lightly browned and springy to the touch.

Cool on a wire rack before eating. These will keep in an airtight container for a couple of days.

# Spelt, hazelnut & honey loaf

I created this loaf because I love the nutty flavour and soft texture that spelt, with its low gluten content, brings to bread. The honey adds a gentle sweetness and the nuts give a little crunch and extra depth. Tempting though it is to eat it straight from the oven, do wait for it to cool. Bread straight from the oven can give you a terrible tummy ache!

### Makes 1 x 900g loaf

500g spelt flour, plus a little extra
   for dusting
10g instant yeast
2 tsp salt
50g hazelnuts, chopped
3 tbsp runny honey
300ml warm water
sunflower oil, for greasing

Place the flour, yeast, salt and chopped hazelnuts in a bowl and stir together, either in a free-standing mixer fitted with the dough hook or by hand. Add the honey and start adding the water – half initially, then around 50ml at a time, bringing in the flour until you have a sticky dough – you may not need all the water. Knead for about 10 minutes (longer if you are kneading by hand), until you have a smooth, elastic dough.

Lightly grease a large mixing bowl, form the dough into a smooth ball and put it in the bowl. Cover with lightly greased cling film and leave to rise somewhere warm for about 1 hour. When the dough has doubled in size tip it out on to a lightly floured work surface and knead gently to knock out any large air bubbles.

Grease and line a 900g loaf tin with baking parchment (or use two 500g tins). The paper is necessary as spelt flour expands in a slightly different way from wheat flour, which can make it difficult to get out of the tin – the paper solves that particular problem!

Put the dough into the prepared tin (or tins), cover with lightly greased cling film and leave to rise again, for around 30 minutes. Meanwhile, preheat the oven to 200°C/Gas 6.

Slash the loaf (or loaves) down the middle with a sharp knife and dust with a little extra flour. Place on the top shelf of the oven, then place a roasting tray half-full of water on the bottom of the oven – the steam created will give the crust a lovely chewy texture. Bake for around 40 minutes (30 if using two smaller tins) then very carefully tip the bread out and put it back in the tin upside down. Return to the oven for a further 5–10 minutes, until browned all over and a tap on the bottom gives a hollow sound. Place on a wire rack and dust with a little more flour. Resist eating until completely cool.

# Cloud bread

During Passover, Jewish people are forbidden from eating bread that has risen, to remember the frantic rush the Jewish slaves were in when they left Egypt with Moses. (Remember the story of Pharaoh and the ten plagues?) This recipe was brought to my attention recently – I realised it is all over the internet thanks to the craze for low-carb eating. It's basically flour-free flatbread. Perfect for Passover – and Kim Kardashian.

## Makes 10–12 pieces

oil, for greasing
3 eggs, separated
3 tbsp full-fat cream cheese
2 tsp runny honey or ½ tsp granulated
   sweetener
½ tsp salt
¼ tsp cream of tartar (or use kosher
   for Passover baking powder)
rosemary sprigs, sesame seeds, chilli flakes
   or nigella seeds, for sprinkling (*optional*)

Preheat the oven to 150°C/Gas 2. Line two baking sheets with baking parchment and grease with oil.

In one bowl, mix together the egg yolks, cream cheese, honey or sweetener and salt until smooth.

In a separate bowl, add the cream of tartar to the egg whites and whisk until you have stiff peaks. You should be able to turn the bowl upside down without incident!

Carefully fold the egg whites into the egg yolk mixture, a spoonful at a time. Try to keep the mixture as light and fluffy as possible.

Place 10–12 spoonfuls of the mixture onto the oiled baking parchment, spacing them a little apart. Sprinkle with your chosen topping, if using, and then bake for 20 minutes until golden brown and set.

Remove from the tray with a spatula and allow to cool on a wire rack before eating.

# Lachoch

Lachoch is a pan-fried Yemenite bread that is like a cross between a pancake and a crumpet. It's full of tiny holes and is brilliant for mopping up soup or dips like hummus. My first experience of it was sitting at table outside a tiny restaurant in the Yemenite Quarter of Tel Aviv. One of the other diners was a Yemenite man who spoke fluent English and told me how to make the bread from memory – he told me he made it to his mother's recipe every week. When I got home I gave it a go – it is great fun and pretty simple. The key is to be patient and cool the pan every time you make one. If the pan isn't cold when the batter goes in, it cooks too quickly and the holes don't have time to form.

**Makes 20**

1kg plain flour
1 tbsp instant yeast
1 tbsp salt
1 tbsp caster sugar
1.5 litres warm water
sunflower oil, for frying

The easiest way to make the batter is to put everything into a blender or food processor and whizz until smooth. Alternatively, mix together the flour, yeast, salt and sugar in a large bowl and make a well in the centre. Gradually pour in the water and stir with a wooden spoon, bringing in the dry ingredients bit by bit until you have a smooth batter. Leave the batter somewhere warm to rise, loosely covered in lightly greased cling film, for 1 hour.

Find a medium non-stick frying pan – one that you would use to make pancakes. Oil it very lightly and wipe off any excess with a piece of kitchen paper. Place the pan over a medium heat and add a ladleful of batter. When it begins to bubble and has set and the base is pale golden, after about 4–5 minutes, slide the lachoch out on to a plate. Cover with a piece of greaseproof paper and prepare to make the next one.

Cool the pan by running the base under cold water. When it is cold, start again – there shouldn't be any need to grease the pan with more oil. Repeat until you have used up all the batter.

The lachoch can be reheated in a low oven or eaten at room temperature. I love them with shakshuka (see page 136) but they are also fantastic – if totally inauthentic – with butter and jam or honey, like a crumpet.

# Courgette & feta loaf

A couple of years ago I was at a dinner for MailOnline where I used to work, and was seated next to the MD of our Australian operation, a terribly nice man called Peter Holder. We started chatting and I told him I had relatives in Sydney. It turned out his partner, Nikki, was one of them! This extraordinary coincidence meant that my twice-yearly business trips to Australia were even more joyful than they might have been because I got to hang out with her and lots of my lovely cousins. It was during one breakfast with Peter and Nikki in a Sydney café that I tried a version of this (typically Aussie) courgette and feta loaf. It's also amazing at teatime, or with a bowl of soup for lunch, as well as topped with eggs or smashed avo at breakfast.

**Makes about 10 slices**

70ml olive oil, plus extra for greasing
250g courgettes
2 eggs, beaten
70g natural yoghurt
100g feta, drained and crumbled
50g cherry tomatoes, quartered
190g self-raising flour
85g ground almonds
½ tsp dried dill
½ tsp dried mint
1 tsp salt
good grinding of black pepper
a small handful of pine nuts, to garnish

Preheat the oven to 180°C/Gas 4 and grease and line a 900g loaf tin with baking parchment.

Grate the courgettes using the large holes on a box grater (or you can use a food processor). Give them a good squeeze to get rid of the excess liquid.

Mix the courgettes, beaten eggs, olive oil, yoghurt, feta and cherry tomatoes together in a bowl. In a separate bowl mix the flour with the ground almonds, dried herbs, salt and pepper. Pour the wet ingredients into the dry and fold gently to combine. Don't overdo it – lumpy is fine – but make sure there are no patches of dry ingredients.

Tip into the prepared loaf tin and shake the tin to level the surface. Sprinkle with pine nuts and bake for 1¼ hours, until golden brown and starting to come away at the edges. You can stick a skewer in the middle to check it is cooked but bear in mind that the tomato and feta will leave wet areas in the loaf. Leave to cool in the tin before turning out and slicing.

# Jessica's pear & ginger bundt

My younger daughter Jessica came home with a pear and ginger cake from her school home economics lesson recently and left it on the kitchen counter to eat gradually over the next few days. I had a taste after she went to bed and it was so delicious that before I knew it I had eaten THE WHOLE THING! How could I not base a cake on something that irresistible?

**Serves 10**

225g butter, softened (or use margarine, for a dairy-free cake), plus extra for greasing
140g caster sugar
140g soft light brown sugar
4 eggs
340g self-raising flour
1 tsp vanilla extract
3 balls of stem ginger from a jar, finely chopped
1 tbsp syrup from the ginger jar
¼ tsp grated nutmeg
½ tsp ground cinnamon
½ tsp salt
1 x 410g tin of pears, drained and finely chopped (240g drained weight)
custard or icing sugar, to serve (*optional*)

Preheat the oven to 190°C/Gas 5. Grease and lightly flour a 23cm bundt tin or grease and line a 23cm round springform cake tin with baking parchment.

Beat the butter with the sugars in a large bowl until light and fluffy, then add the eggs one by one, beating after each addition and adding a tablespoon of flour with each egg to prevent curdling. Beat in the vanilla extract, chopped ginger and ginger syrup.

Mix the rest of the flour in a bowl with the nutmeg, cinnamon and salt. Fold the dry mixture into the wet mixture and then fold through the chopped pears.

Pour into the prepared tin and bake for 1 hour, until golden brown and a skewer inserted into the centre comes out clean. Leave to cool in the tin for 10 minutes, then turn out on to a wire rack.

Serve warm as a dessert with custard or cold as a cake scattered with icing sugar and with a good cup of tea.

 Variation:

*Replace the ginger with 100g dark chocolate chips and use 1 tablespoon of juice from the tinned pears instead of the ginger syrup.*

# Orange, walnut & olive oil cake

This is a gorgeous dairy-free cake, making it a perfect dessert option for observant Jews who will not mix meat and milk in a meal. I love it with the sliced oranges on page 212, but if eating dairy isn't an issue, it's also delicious with a scoop of ice cream or a dollop of crème fraîche, or just with a cup of strong coffee. I do love an easy-to-make, multi-tasking cake — this is one of my favourites.

## Serves 10–12

120ml olive oil, plus extra for greasing
360g plain flour, plus extra for dusting
125g ground walnuts (or use chopped
   walnuts and pulse in a food processor
   until ground)
½ tsp ground cinnamon
½ tsp ground cloves
grated zest and juice of 2 oranges
   (you need about 180ml juice)
2 tsp baking powder
½ tsp salt
2 eggs, beaten
200g soft light brown sugar
1 tsp vanilla extract
icing sugar, for dusting

Preheat the oven to 190°C/Gas 5. Grease a 22cm round springform cake tin with a little olive oil and dust with flour, shaking away the excess. (You can also use a bundt tin if you prefer. I always prefer a bundt tin.)

In a bowl, mix together the flour, ground walnuts, cinnamon, cloves, orange zest, baking powder and salt.

In a second bowl or jug, mix together the orange juice, olive oil, beaten eggs, brown sugar and vanilla extract. Pour the wet mixture into the dry mixture and combine until there are no patches of dry ingredients (a lumpy mixture is fine). Pour into the prepared tin.

Bake for 45 minutes, until a skewer inserted into the centre comes out clean, then allow to cool in the tin for 15 minutes before removing and cooling fully on a wire rack. Dust with icing sugar before cutting into slices.

# Lemon date squares

This is another recipe from my sister-in-law Sarah and it has become a real favourite of mine. They're the kind of thing I like to make on a Sunday and have around for when the girls get in after school or if friends pop in. They've got dates in them so they're super–healthy, right?

**Makes 12**

FOR THE LEMON DATE FILLING
350g pitted dates
175ml water
grated zest and juice of 1 lemon
¼ tsp salt

FOR THE CRUST
180g porridge oats
120g wholemeal flour
½ tsp bicarbonate of soda
¼ tsp salt
160ml maple syrup
120ml sunflower oil
1 tsp vanilla extract

Preheat the oven to 180°C/Gas 4 and line a 20cm square brownie tin with baking parchment (or use a non-stick tin).

Place the dates in a small pan with the water, the lemon zest and juice and salt. Cook over a medium heat for about 5 minutes, stirring regularly, until the dates break down and the mixture becomes smooth. Remove from the heat.

For the crust, put the oats, flour, bicarbonate of soda and salt in a bowl and mix well. In a separate bowl, mix together the maple syrup, sunflower oil and vanilla and add to the dry ingredients. Stir well.

Tip three-quarters of the crust mixture into the brownie tin and press the mixture evenly into the corners. Pour the date filling on top and then sprinkle the remaining crust mixture on top of the date filling.

Bake for 25 minutes, until golden brown. Allow to cool completely in the tin before cutting into squares.

# Persian love cake

There are various versions of the story behind this cake but they all start thus: a girl bakes a cake to win the heart of a Persian prince. The ending can go one of two ways – in the tragic version, he has a fatal allergy to saffron and drops dead. I'm more comfortable with the happy-ever-after alternative. Either way, this cake is phenomenal. It contains all my favourite things – pistachios, cardamom, saffron, almonds, rose water, orange zest – and I really can't recommend strongly enough that you bake it RIGHT NOW. And send me a big slice.

**Serves 10**

300g unsalted butter, softened, plus extra
   for greasing
a pinch of saffron strands
grated zest of 1 orange, plus 2 tbsp
   orange juice
300g caster sugar
4 eggs
2 tsp rose water
seeds from 5 cardamom pods
½ tsp mixed spice
200g self-raising flour
½ tsp baking powder
60g pistachios, ground in a spice grinder
   or food processor to a coarse powder
60g ground almonds
a pinch of salt

FOR THE BUTTERCREAM
100g full-fat cream cheese
50g unsalted butter, softened
300g icing sugar
½ tsp rose water
1 or 2 drops of red food colouring

TO DECORATE
pistachios, lightly crushed
dried rose petals (*optional*)

Preheat the oven to 180°C/Gas 4 and grease and line the base of three 15cm round cake tins with baking parchment.

Soak the saffron strands in the 2 tablespoons of orange juice for a few minutes. Meanwhile, cream the butter and sugar in a bowl until creamy and pale then add the eggs, one at a time, beating well after each addition. Add the orange zest, rose water, cardamom seeds and mixed spice and beat again, then add the soaked saffron and orange juice, too. Fold in the flour, baking powder, ground pistachios, ground almonds and salt.

Divide the mixture evenly between the three tins and bake for 25 minutes until golden, risen and starting to come away from the sides of the tin. A skewer inserted into the centre should come out clean. Leave to cool in the tins while you make the rose buttercream.

Making the buttercream is easiest if you just put everything in a food processor and whizz to a smooth, fluffy frosting with the palest pink hue, but you can also make it using a handheld electric mixer: start by mixing the cream cheese and butter together, then whisk in the icing sugar and finally add the rose water and one or two drops of red food colouring to make it a pale pink colour.

To assemble the cake, sandwich the layers with two-thirds of the buttercream. Spread the remaining buttercream over the top, then sprinkle with crushed pistachios and dried rose petals, if using.

# Tahini & date brownies

These are seriously grown-up brownies. Not that kids don't like them, but the muskiness of the tahini with the dark chocolate makes these suitable for the most sophisticated gatherings as well as for a teatime treat. Serve them warm for dessert, topped with vanilla ice cream, sprinkled with sesame seeds and drizzled with more date syrup — which you can now buy in supermarkets as well as in Middle Eastern stores. Or, of course, just guzzle one with a cup of coffee.

## Makes 16

140g salted butter, cubed, plus extra
   for greasing
200g dark chocolate, broken into squares
200g caster sugar
a pinch of salt
2 eggs, plus 1 egg yolk
10 plump pitted dates, chopped into small
   pieces (medjool are ideal)
85g plain flour
2 tbsp date syrup (*silan*)
3 tbsp tahini

Preheat the oven to 180°C/Gas 4. Grease a 20cm square brownie tin and line with baking parchment, leaving an overhang so you can remove it easily later.

Melt the chocolate and butter in a bowl set over a pan of simmering water, making sure the bottom of the bowl doesn't touch the water. Remove from the heat and stir, then whisk in the sugar, salt, eggs and egg yolk and chopped dates. Fold in the flour.

Pour into the lined tin then drizzle over the date syrup and tahini — if your tahini is a bit too thick, loosen it with a splash of water. Use a skewer to swirl interesting patterns in the mixture. (Please note: this does not need you to be artistic. A few swirls is fine.)

Bake for 35 minutes, until the top has started to crack and you can feel a firmness when you press gently on the top. You don't want them to be too hard — a bit of squish in the middle is perfect. Allow to cool in the tin, then cut into squares.

 ## Variation:

*For the most incredibly decadent chocolate orange brownies, omit the dates, tahini and date syrup. Pour half the brownie mixture into the tin, lay Terry's Dark Chocolate Orange slices over the top (you will need 16 slices, around three-quarters of an orange) and cover with the remaining brownie mix. Scatter with candied orange zest and bake as above.*

# Coconut & chocolate flapjacks

Flapjacks are a constant in my kitchen – partly because we always seem to have the ingredients to hand but also because they are one of the first things my daughters could make themselves and, since they have oats in them, I can pretend that they are a healthier teatime treat. This version came about because I love the combination of coconut and chocolate. After I made the first batch I took them into work to see how they went down. They got rave reviews and loads of requests for the recipe. So here it is!

**Makes 12**

115g salted butter
115g soft light brown sugar
3 tbsp golden syrup or date syrup (*silan*)
2 tbsp cocoa powder
225g porridge oats
40g dried cranberries
40g raisins
50g desiccated coconut

Preheat the oven to 180°C/Gas 4 and line a 20cm square brownie tin with baking parchment (or use a non-stick tin).

Put the butter, brown sugar, syrup and cocoa powder into a pan and melt together over a medium heat. Stir well, remove from the heat and add the remaining ingredients. Stir to combine and then press into the prepared tin.

Bake in the oven for 20 minutes. Allow to cool in the tin, before cutting into 12 bars.

# Fruity tea loaf

When I was little, back in the seventies, my mum was always trying out the latest fad diets and at one stage went totally fat-free. A jug of reconstituted, powdered, skimmed milk resided miserably in the bottom of the fridge (you couldn't buy skimmed milk in bottles then), mayonnaise was suddenly replaced with low-fat salad cream, jacket potatoes had no butter or cheese on them. . . but there was one wonderful saving grace: this tea loaf. Yes, it's full of sugar and dates and sultanas and even booze (though to be fair, that was a later addition by me) but it is fat free so back then it was a regular fixture at teatime. I have changed the original recipe quite a lot – it now has extra spice, orange zest and a variety of fruit, as well as muscovado sugar to give it a satisfyingly sticky texture. I always make two at once because it lasts really well for a week or so if wrapped up tightly in foil but feel free to halve the recipe if you like. My advice is to have a thick slice slathered in not remotely fat-free, but good-quality, lightly salted butter, with a cup of tea.

## Makes 2 x 900g loaves

300g muscovado sugar
2 tea bags brewed with 500ml boiling water
100ml dark rum
200g raisins
400g mixed dried fruit (I use whatever
    I have to hand, such as dates, dried figs,
    mixed peel, glacé cherries, dried apricots,
    dried apples etc.)
400g plain flour
2 tsp baking powder
2 tsp mixed spice
a good grating of nutmeg
grated zest of 1 orange
2 eggs, beaten

Put the sugar in a bowl, pour over the tea and stir to dissolve. Add the rum, raisins and all the dried fruit (leaving the pieces whole). Leave to soak for at least 30 minutes and overnight if you like.

When you are ready to bake, preheat the oven to 180°C/Gas 4 and line two 900g loaf tins with baking parchment.

Mix together the flour, baking powder, mixed spice, nutmeg and orange zest in a large bowl. And the soaked fruit mixture and the beaten eggs and mix well. Pour into the loaf tins and bake for 1¼ hours, or until the loaves are golden brown and well risen and a skewer inserted into the middle of each loaf comes out with just a few crumbs sticking to it (rather than uncooked cake mix).

Allow to cool in the tins for a few minutes before turning out on to a wire rack to cool completely.

# Index

# Acknowledgements

Thank you so much to:

Jane Finigan, my adorable and incredibly talented agent at Lutyens and Rubinstein; Muna Reyal, my publisher at Headline, who has held my hand every step of the way, ever confident in me even when I wibbled; Emma Lee, the most amazing photographer who sees the beauty in everything and makes everything look stunning; Laura Herring, who is the most wonderful, organised, patient and skillful editor, whose joyous emails always make me smile; Joss Herd, who has made all my recipes look gorgeous and is really great at doing jumping press-ups (don't try this at home); Tabitha Hawkins, who indulges my love of blue plates, is a genius with a piece of wood and a paintbrush and never stops smiling; Nikki Dupin, an amazing designer who has made this book look SO pretty; and Mitzie Wilson, who tested my recipes and gave such helpful and positive suggestions for improvement. Also at Headline, thank you to Kate Miles for her editorial help, Sarah Badhan in production and Katie Brown in publicity.

To my team and bosses at MailOnline who gave me so much support while I juggled so much. And to everyone who shared, tested and tasted the recipes here.

To Nikola Bartekova, who looked after everything at home while I gallivanted around and who makes a great Friday night dinner – you are a truly special young woman and we have been so lucky to have you in our lives.

And to my family – the Levys, the Shooters and the Raanans. You are the most supportive, affectionate, ever-hungry, generous, noisy, emotional bunch anyone could have in their lives and I adore you all.

Charlotte and Jessica: this book is really for you to use when you are old enough to have your own families and cook for them. Don't follow the recipes too closely. Do your own thing, always. Sing your own song, dance your own dance and do everything you ever dreamed you might do.

Dan, I would be lost without you by my side. Thank you for everything.

**Anne Shooter** has been a journalist for 20 years, mainly at the *Daily Mail* and **MailOnline** and has also written for titles including *delicious. magazine*, the *Jewish Chronicle*, the *Guardian* and *Woman & Home.*

Anne's love of cooking also led her to complete the Leiths School of Food and Wine's professional diploma and as such she also caters events and hosts numerous noisy dinner parties for as many friends and relatives as she can, whenever she has time.

Her first book, *Sesame & Spice: Baking from the East End to the Middle East*, was nominated for the Guild of Food Writers' First Book Award.

She lives in London with her husband Dan, daughters Charlotte and Jessica, and labradoodle Rufus.

Hardback ISBN 978 1 4722 4319 5
eISBN 978 1 4722 4321 8

Commissioning Editor: Muna Reyal
Project Editor: Laura Herring
Design: Nikki Dupin
Photography: Emma Lee
Food styling: Joss Herd
Prop styling: Tabitha Hawkins
Copy editor: Clare Sayer
Proofreader: Laura Nickoll
Indexer: Cathy Heath

Colour origination by Born
Printed and bound in China

HEADLINE PUBLISHING GROUP
Carmelite House
50 Victoria Embankment
London EC4Y 0DZ

www.headline.co.uk
www.hachette.co.uk